Thank you for your purchase!!

Mandala Mania Volume 2 is a teen to adult coloring book designed to quiet your mind by helping you focus. Created to help provide relaxation and stress relief, this book delivers hours of satisfying, entertaining fun while allowing you to express your innermost creative self. The drawings offer a nice range in detail and complexity allowing hours of enjoyment for everyone from beginners to experts.

The complex designs are all printed single sided to help prevent any color bleeding from one picture to another. However, if you are using markers, we do suggest that you place a single sheet of blank paper behind the page you are coloring.

If you enjoy your coloring experience please show your appreciation by leaving us a review. We would also love to see a picture of how your art has turned out!!

Mandala Mania

Volume 2

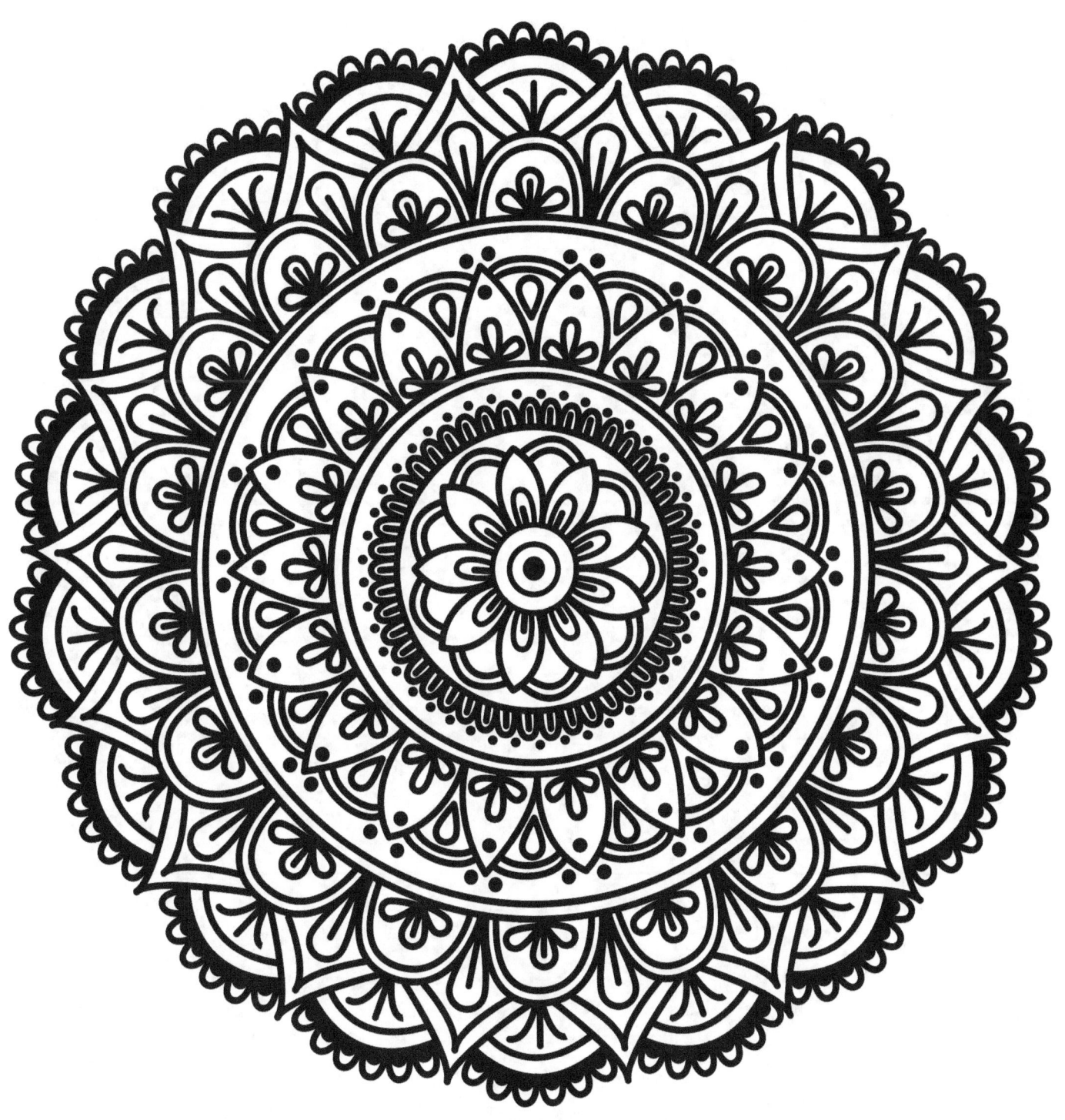

This book belongs to

_____

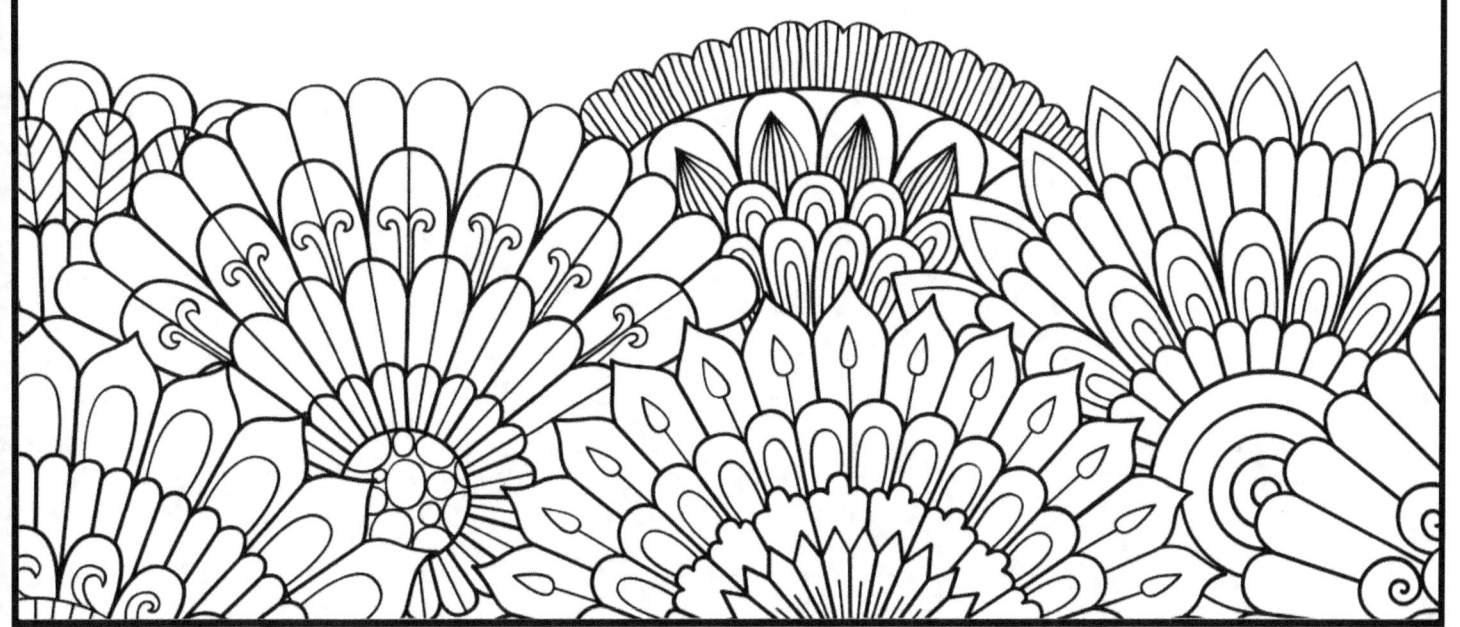

Color Testing

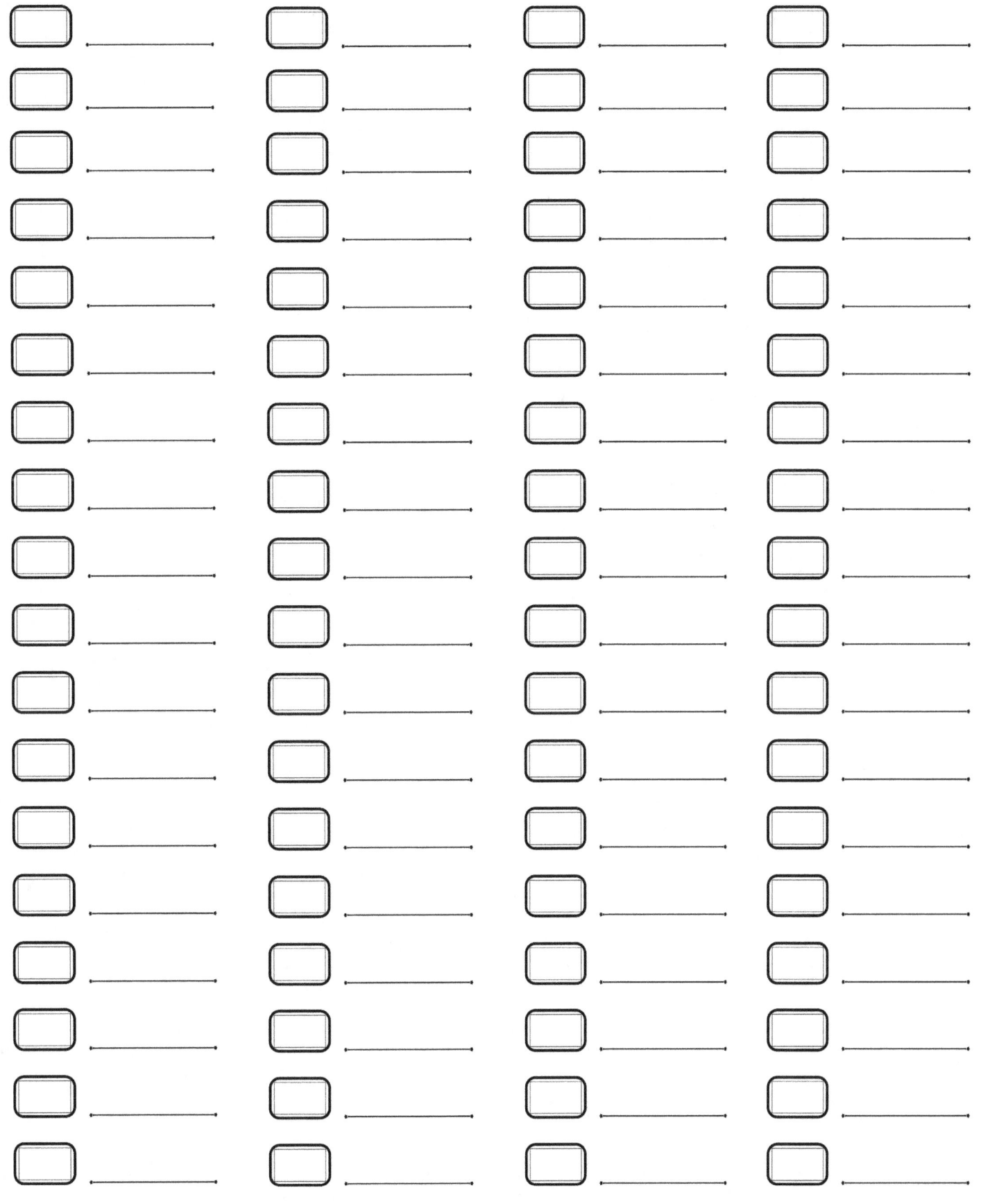

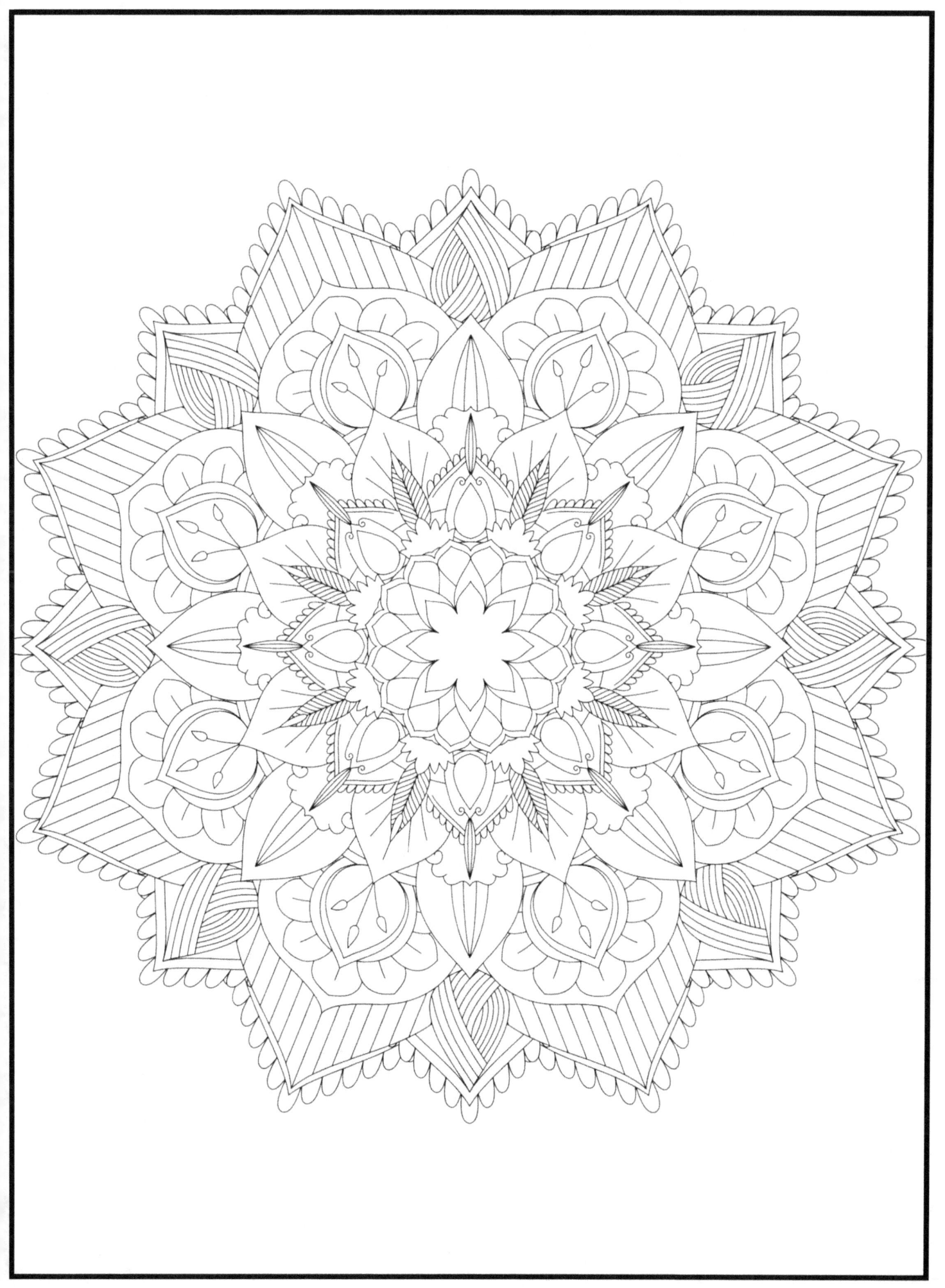

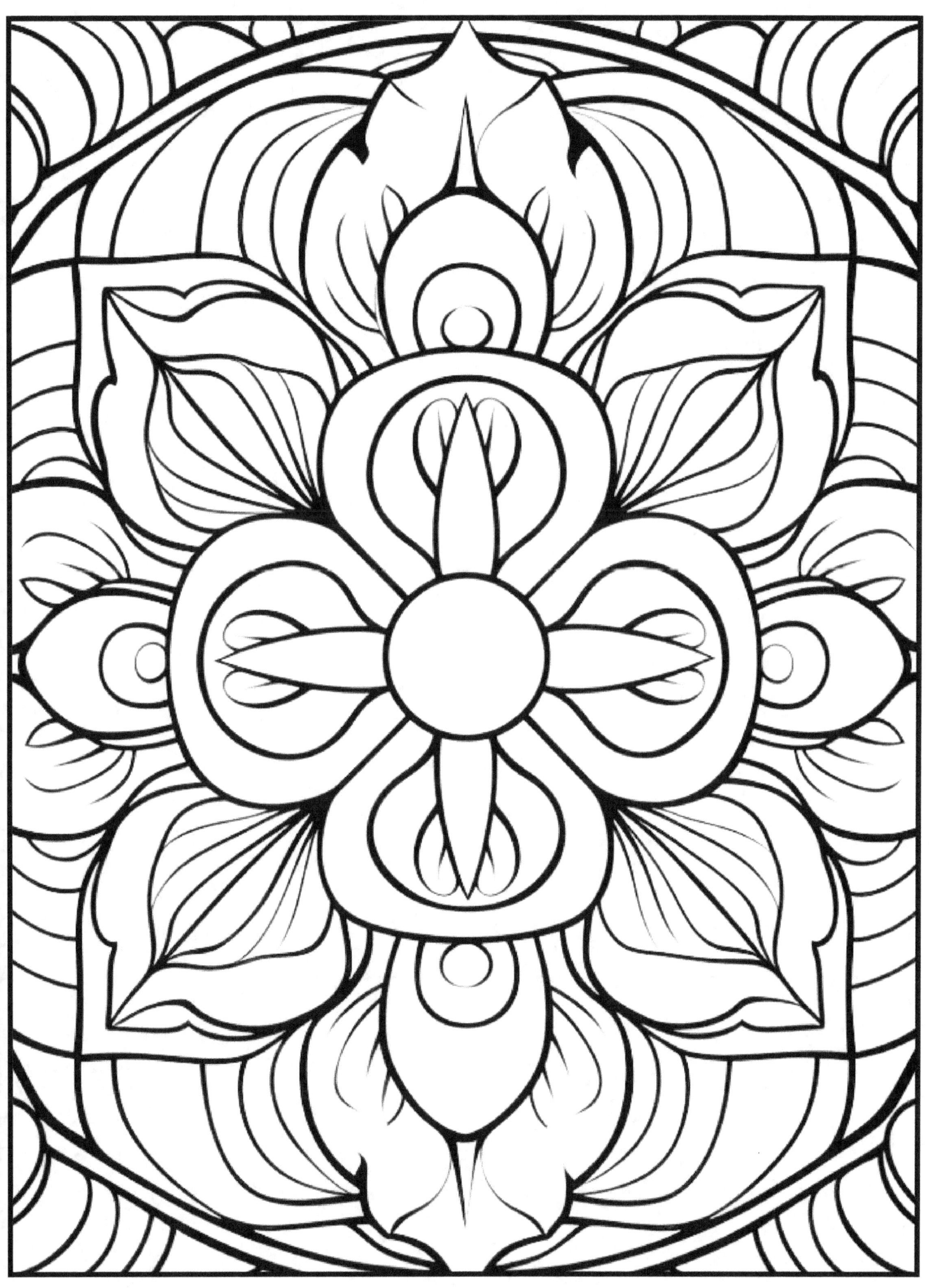

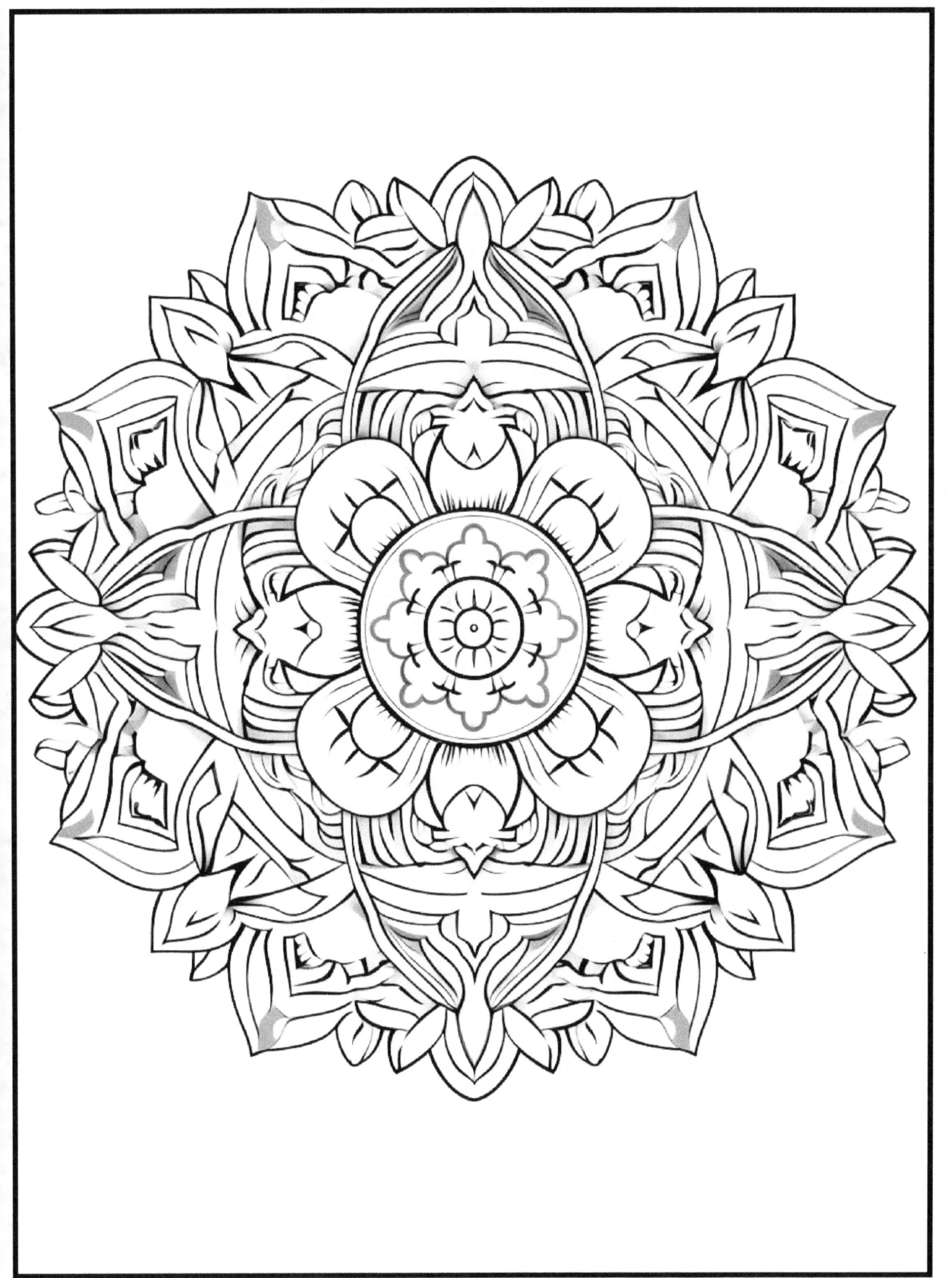

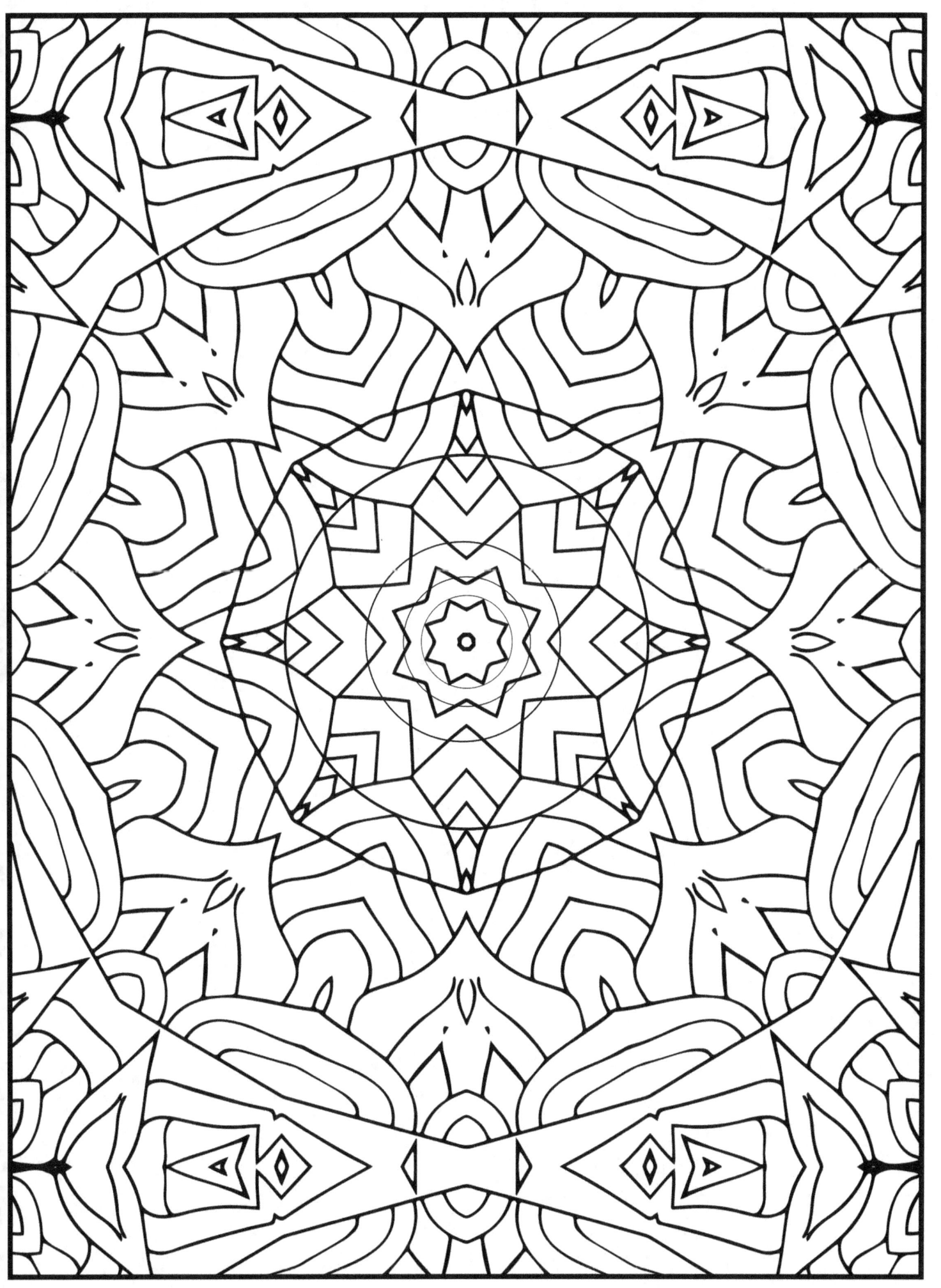

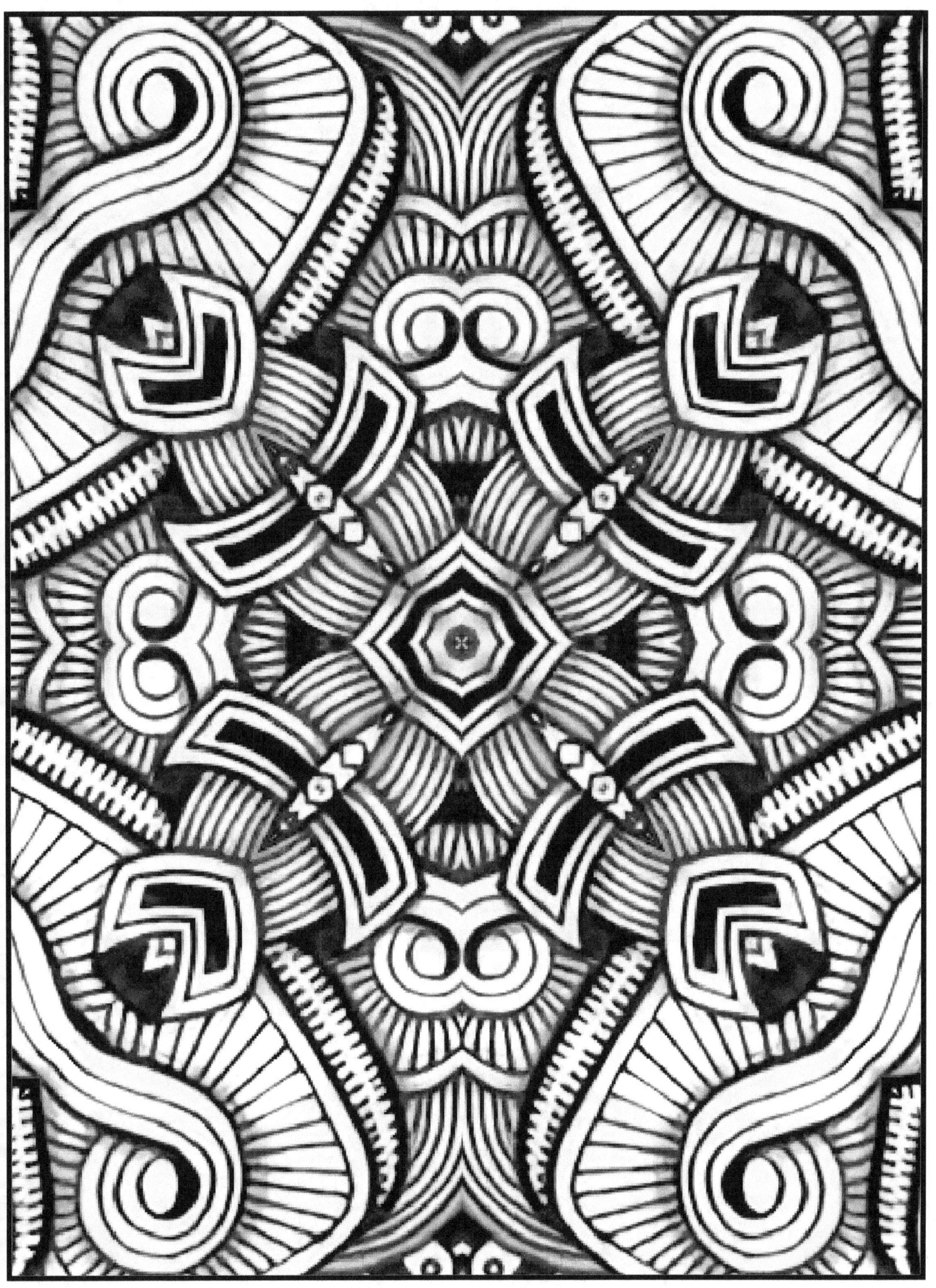

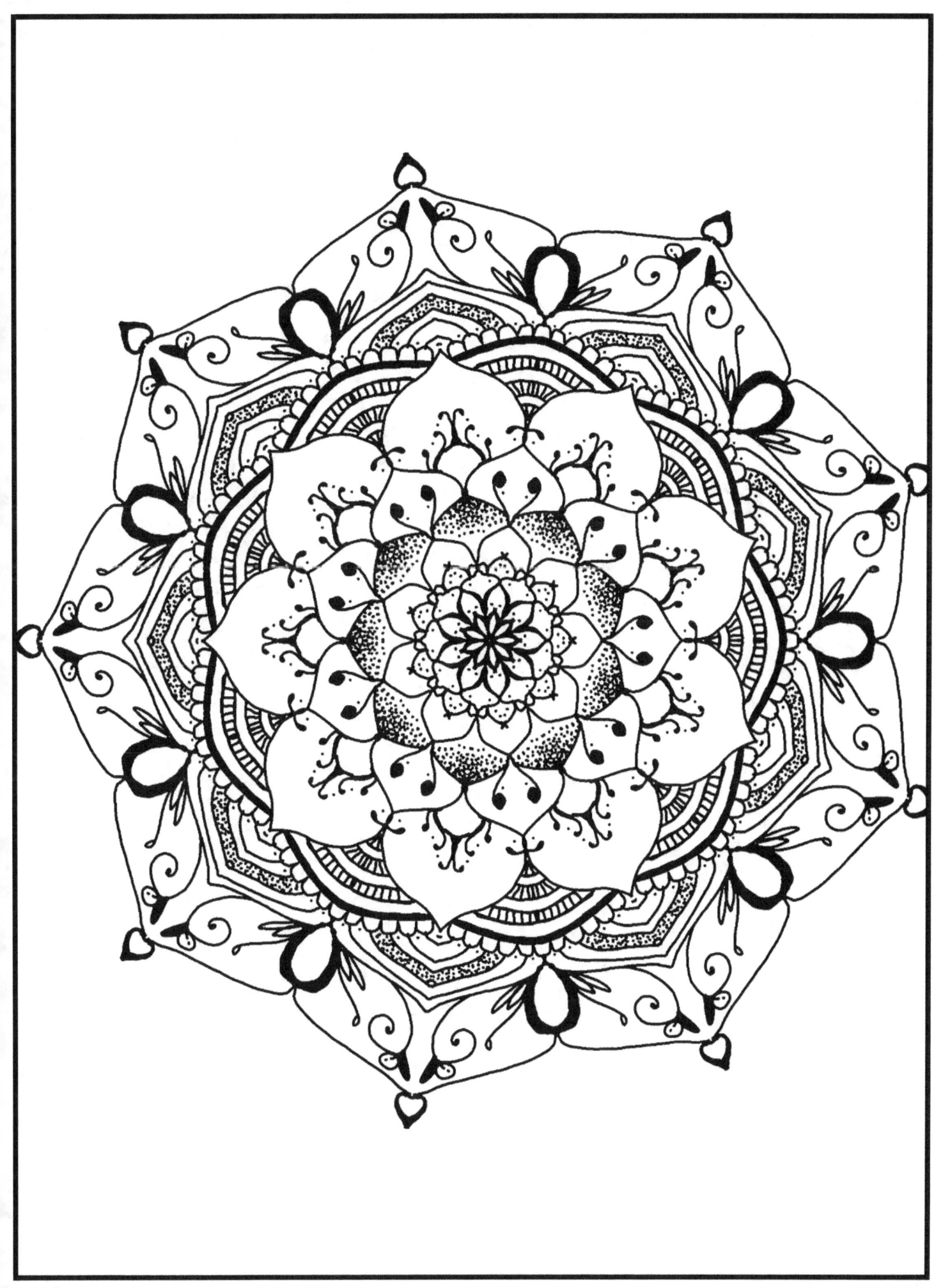

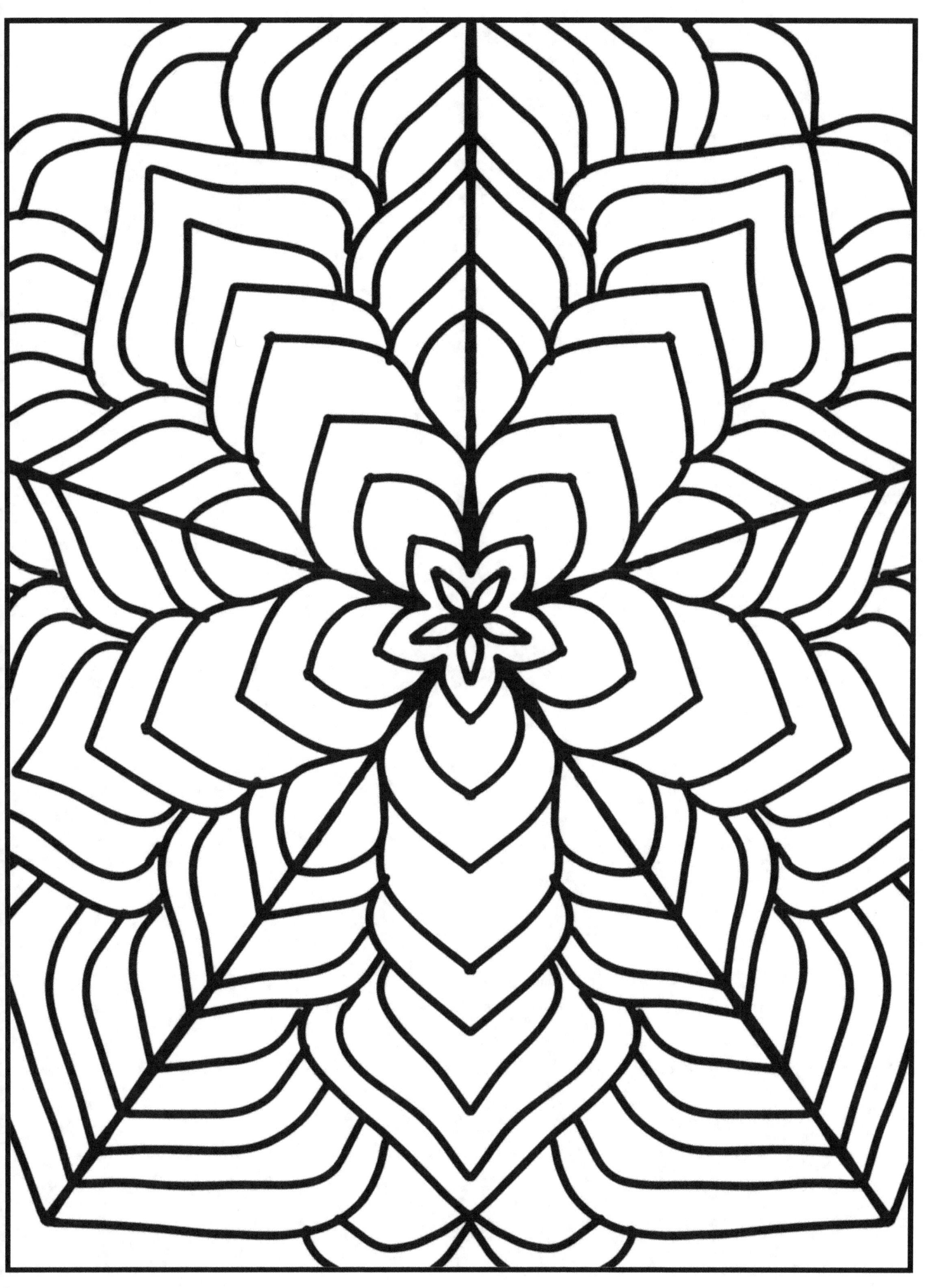

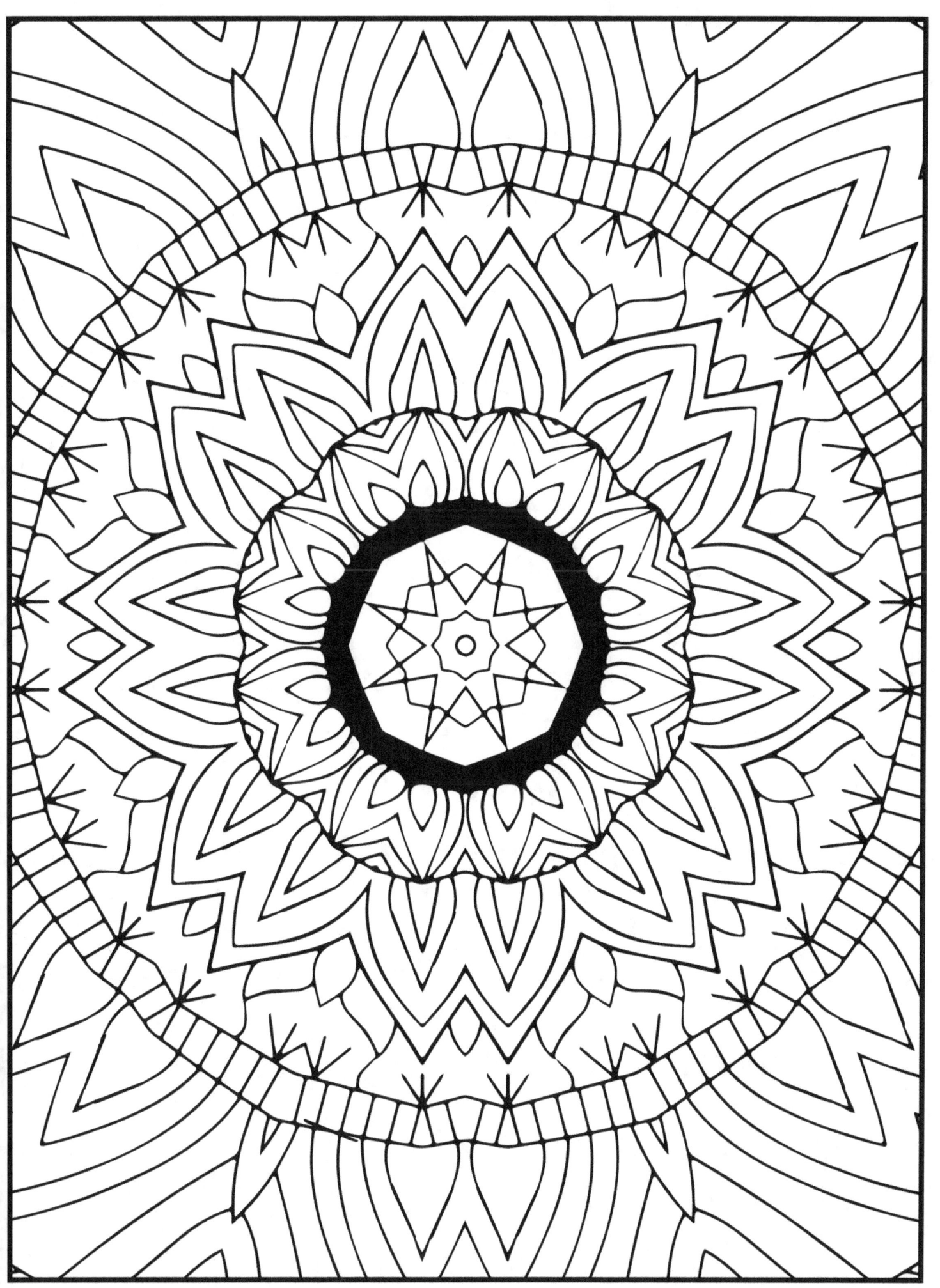

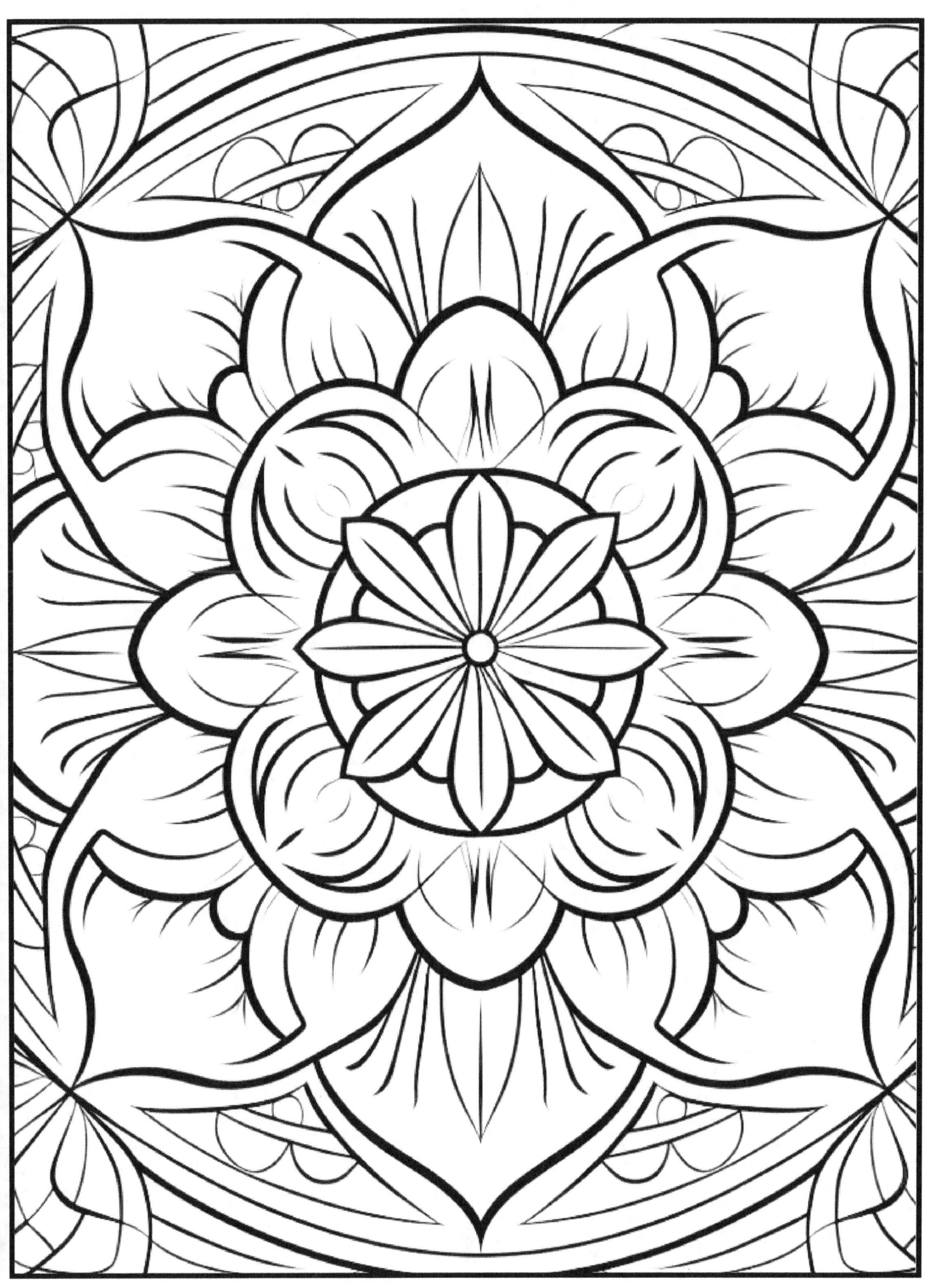

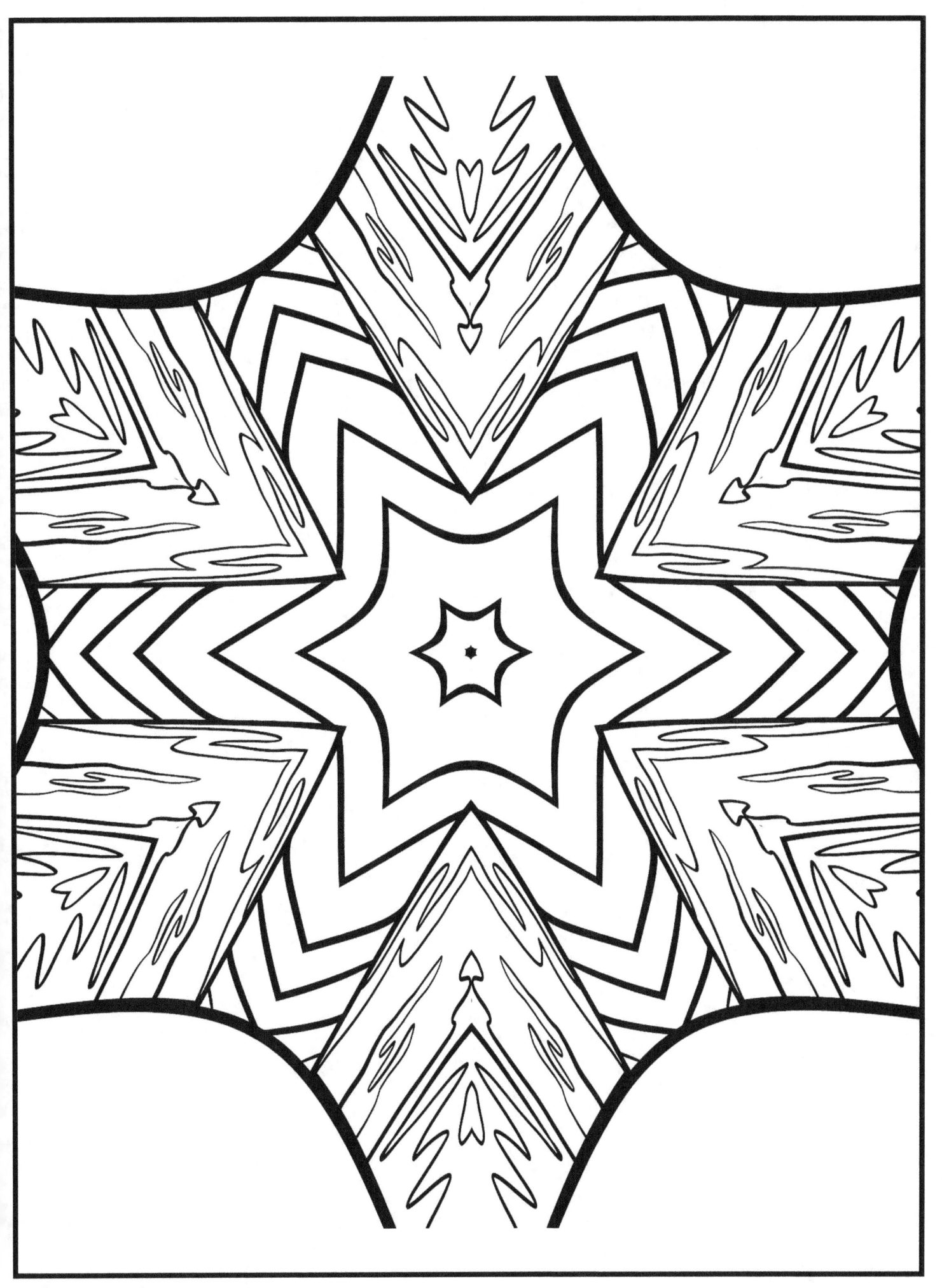

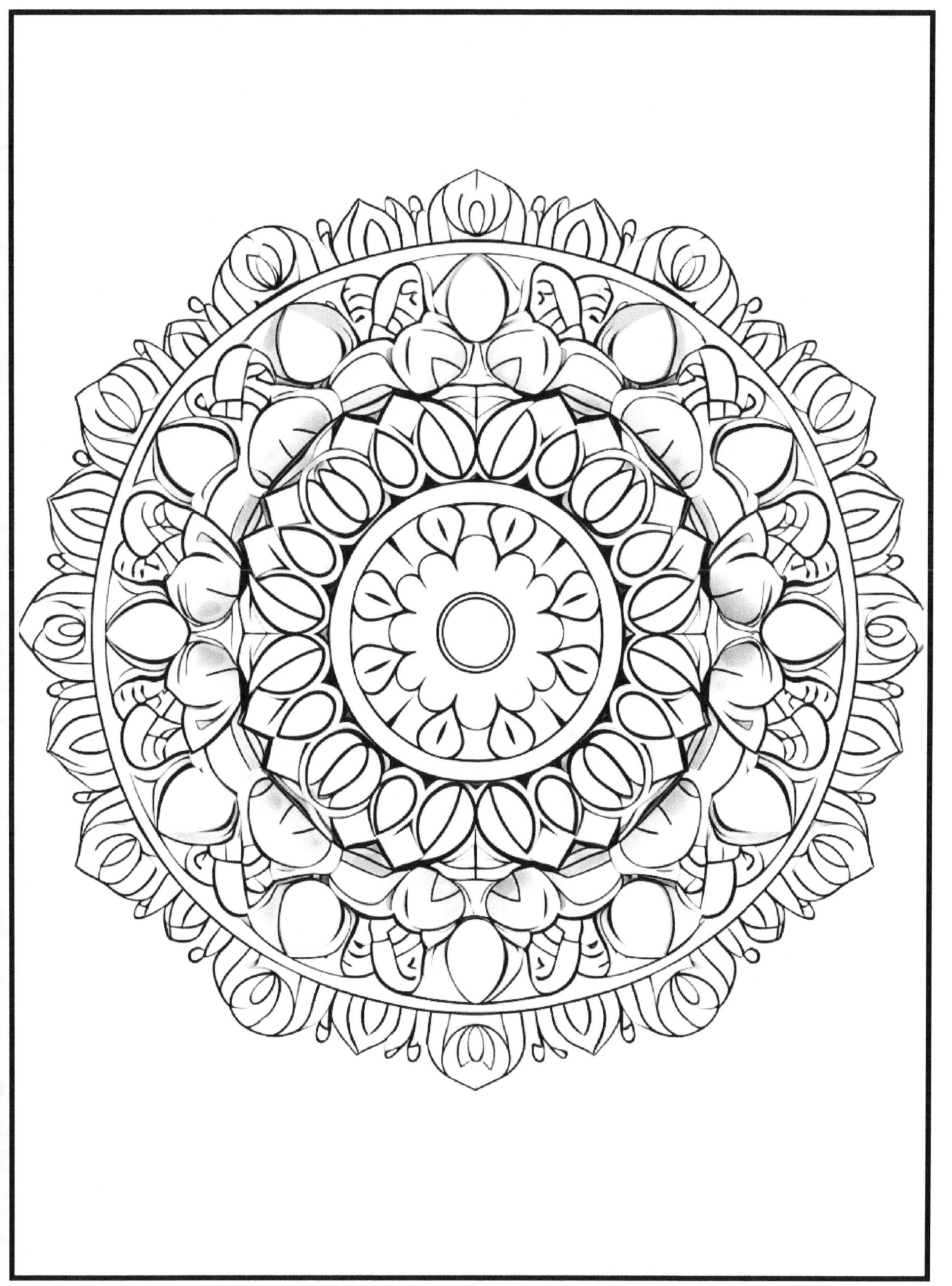

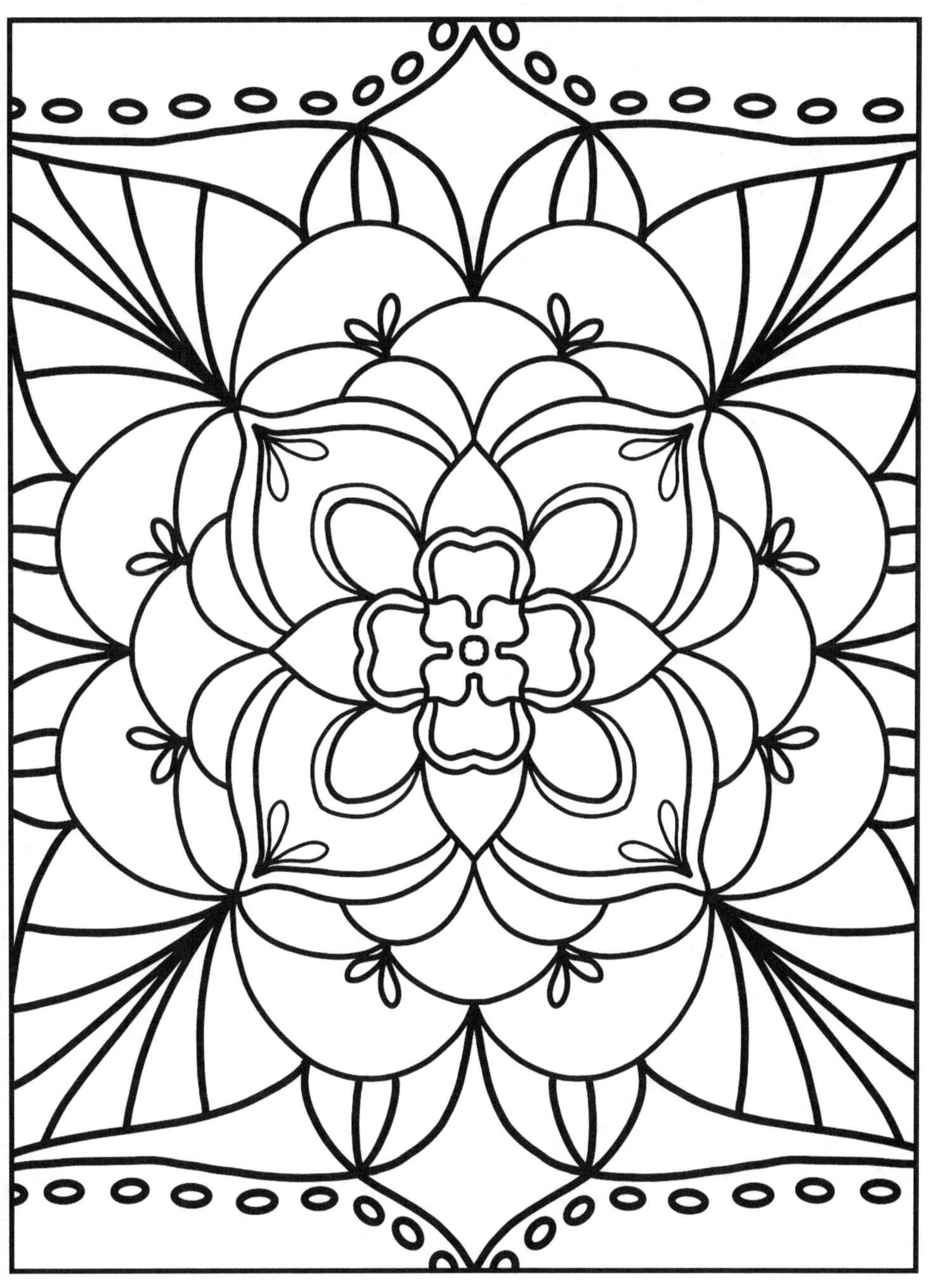

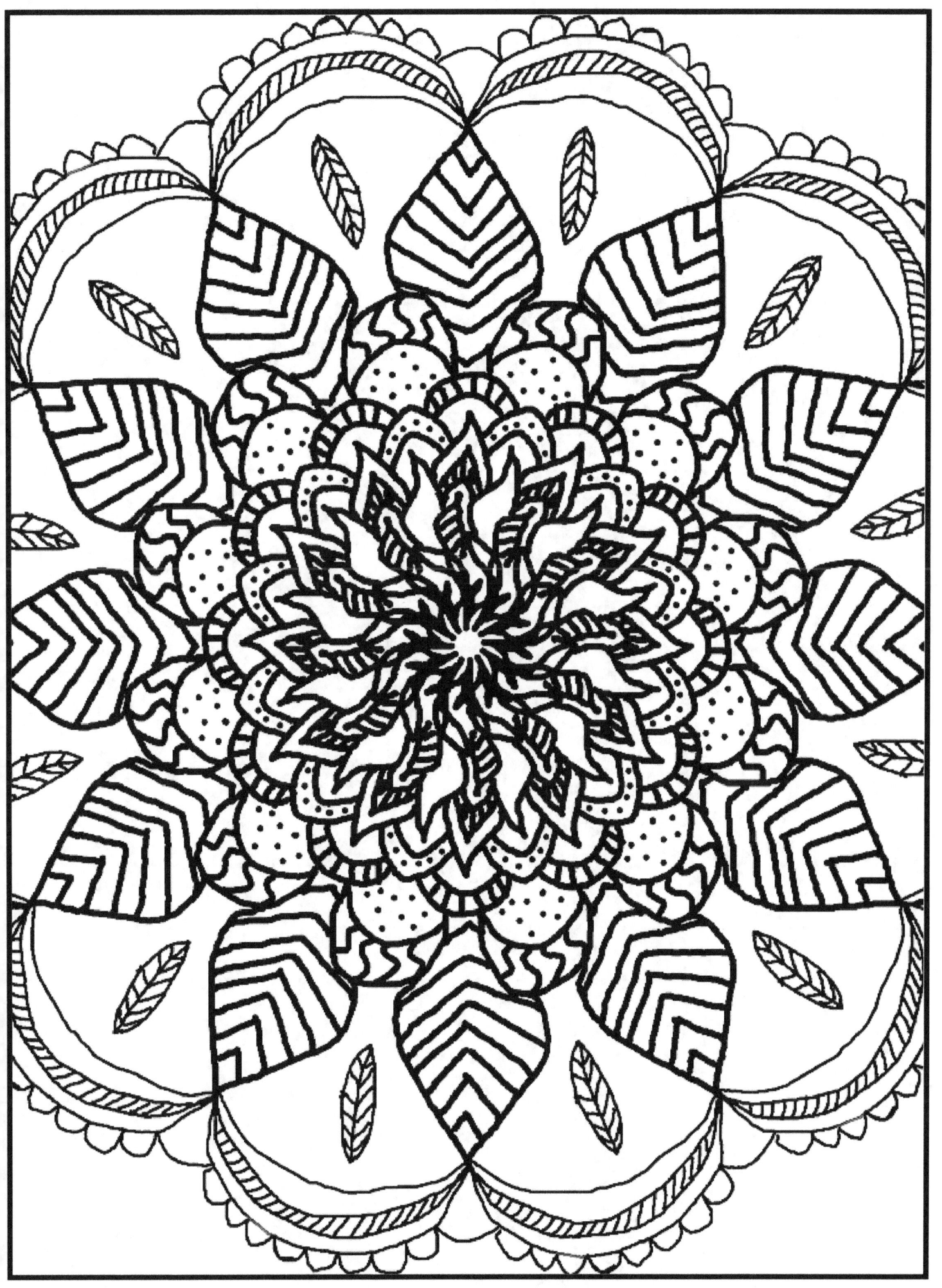

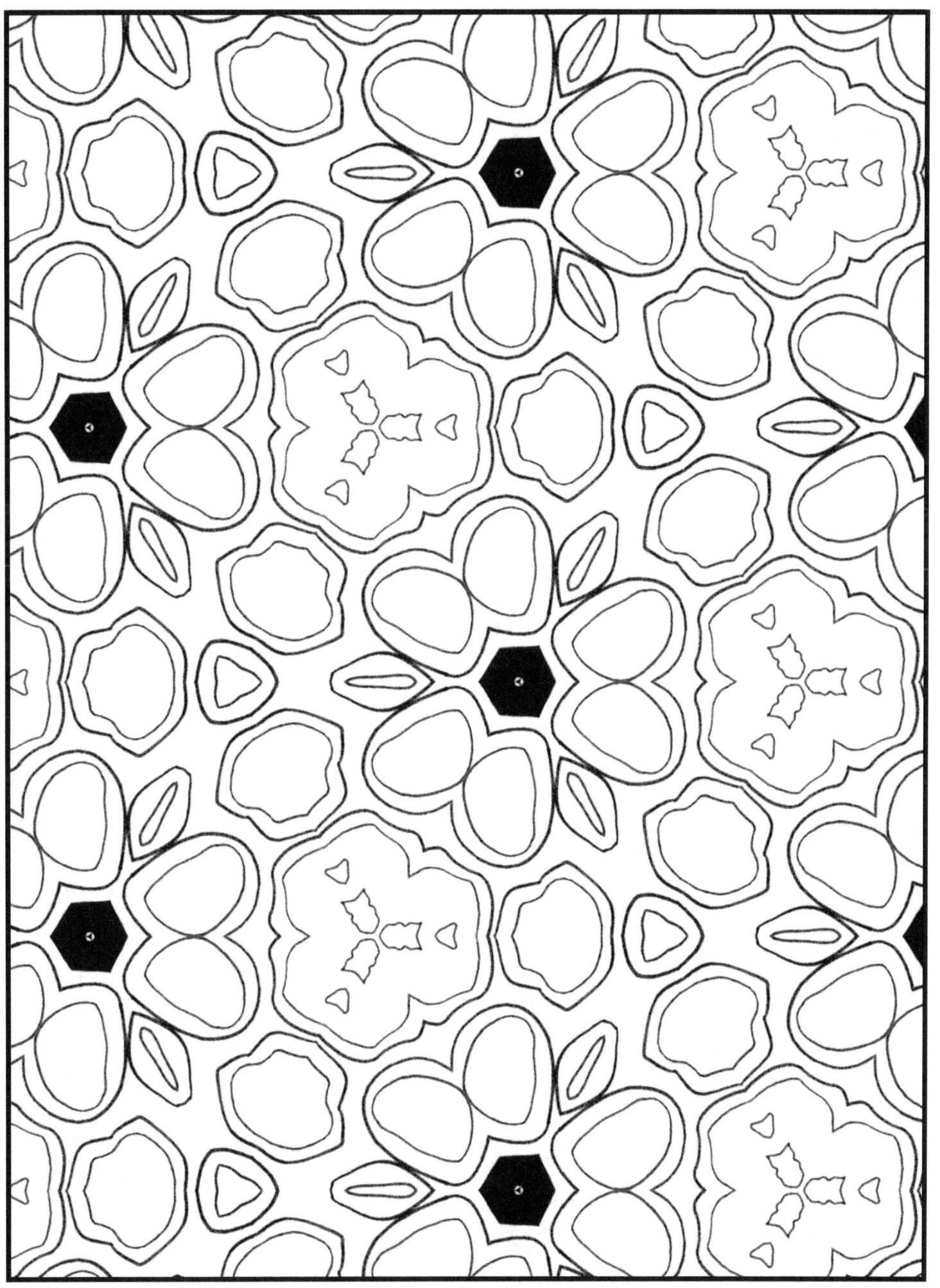

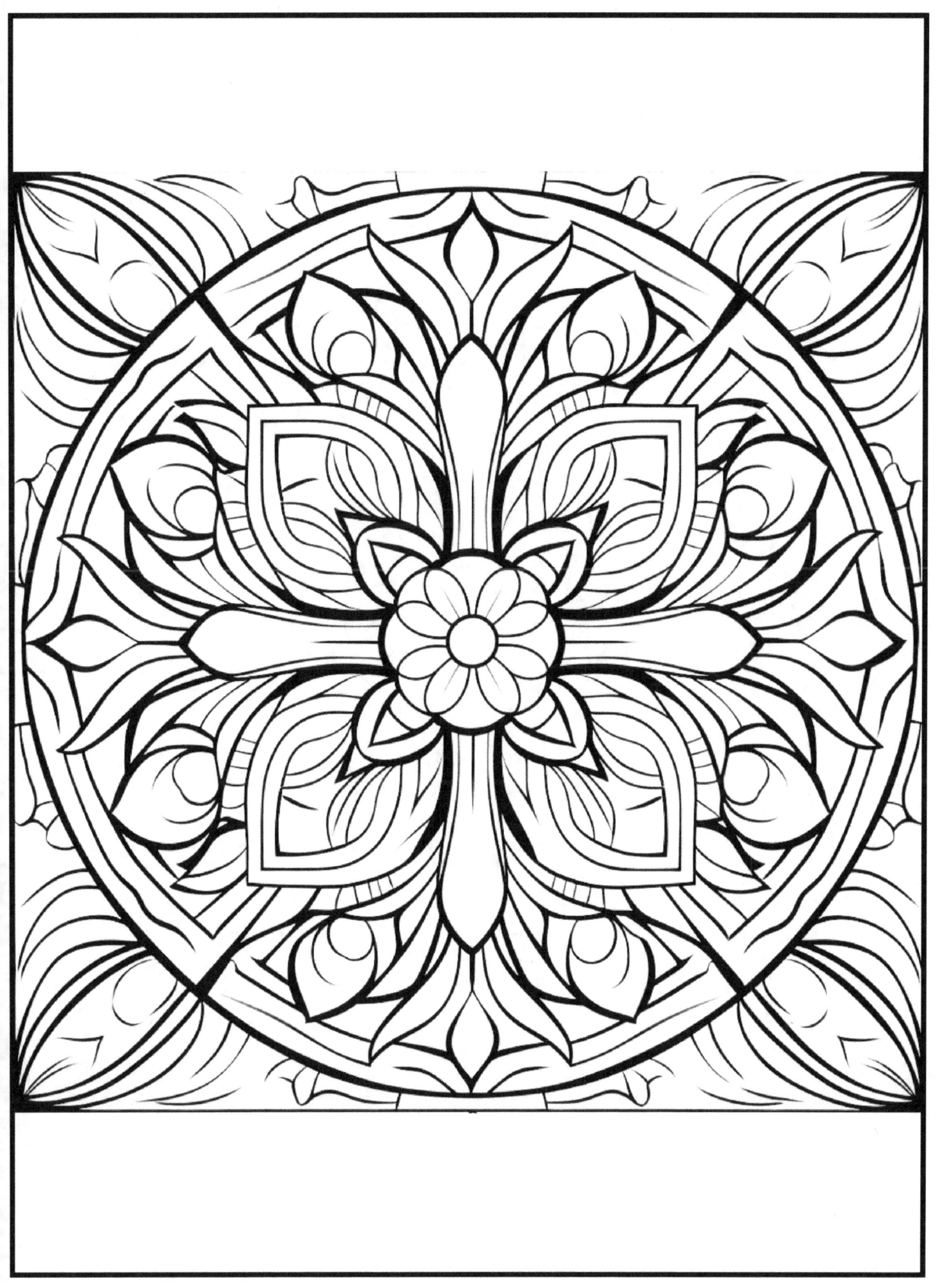

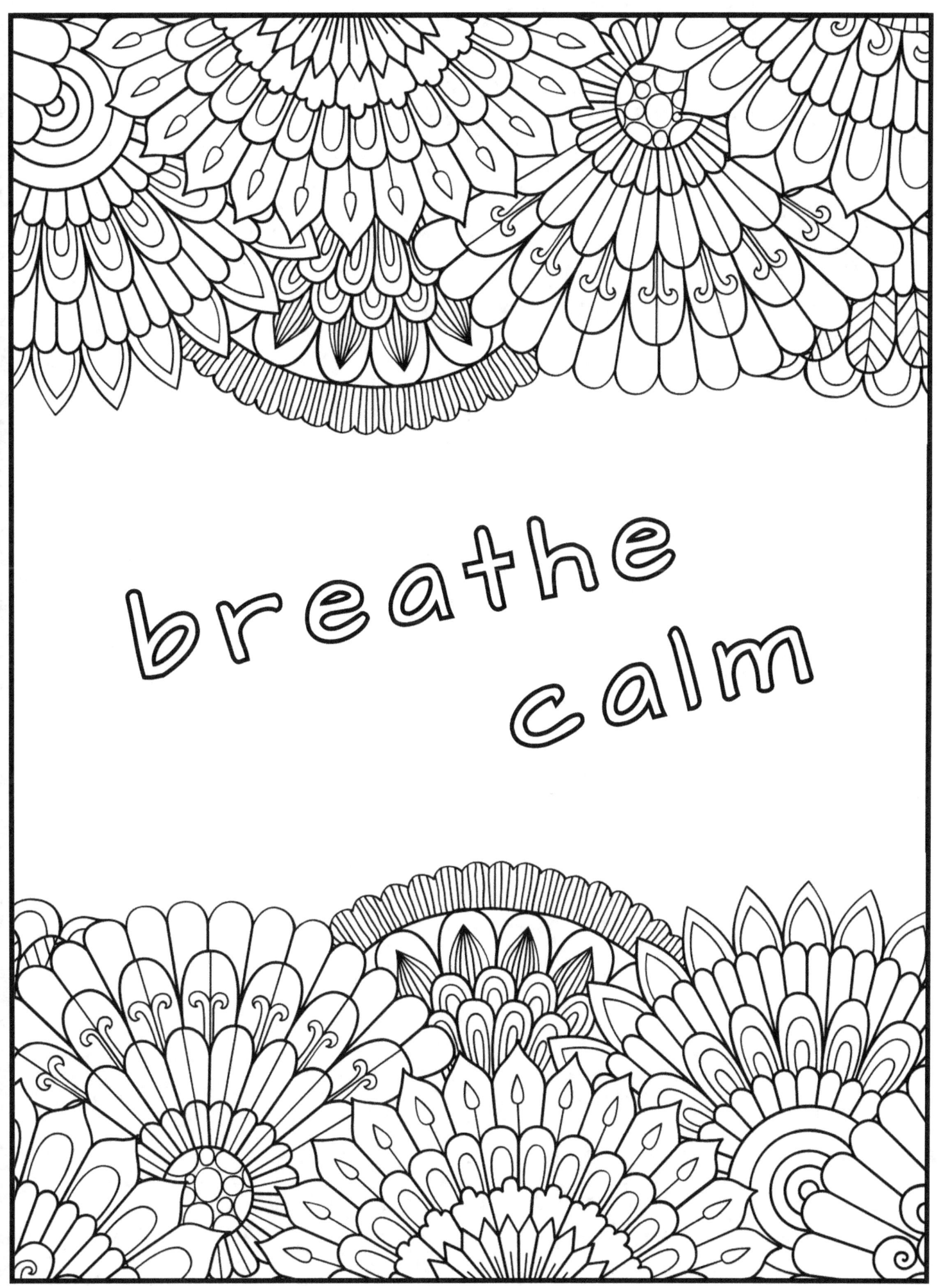

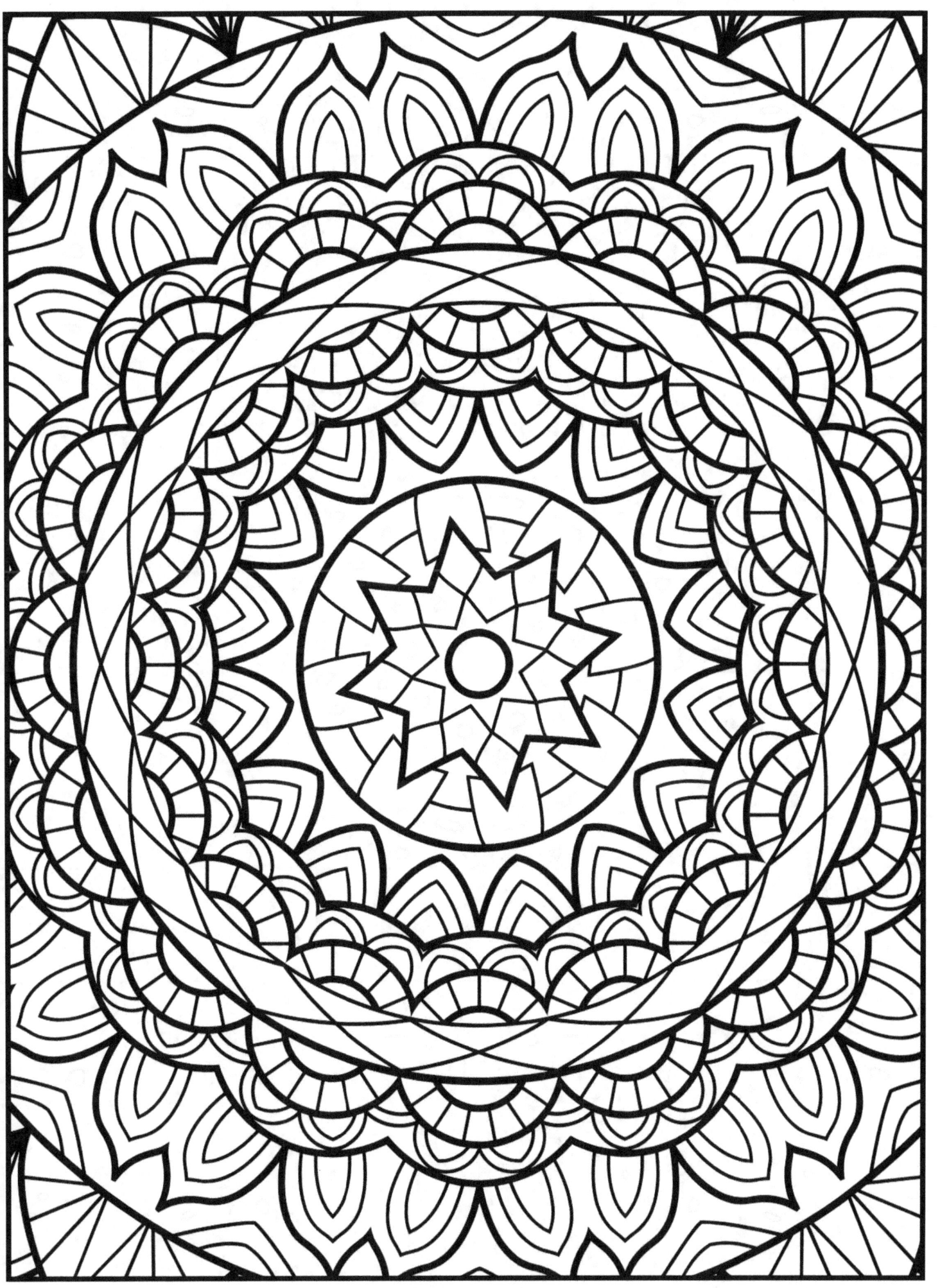

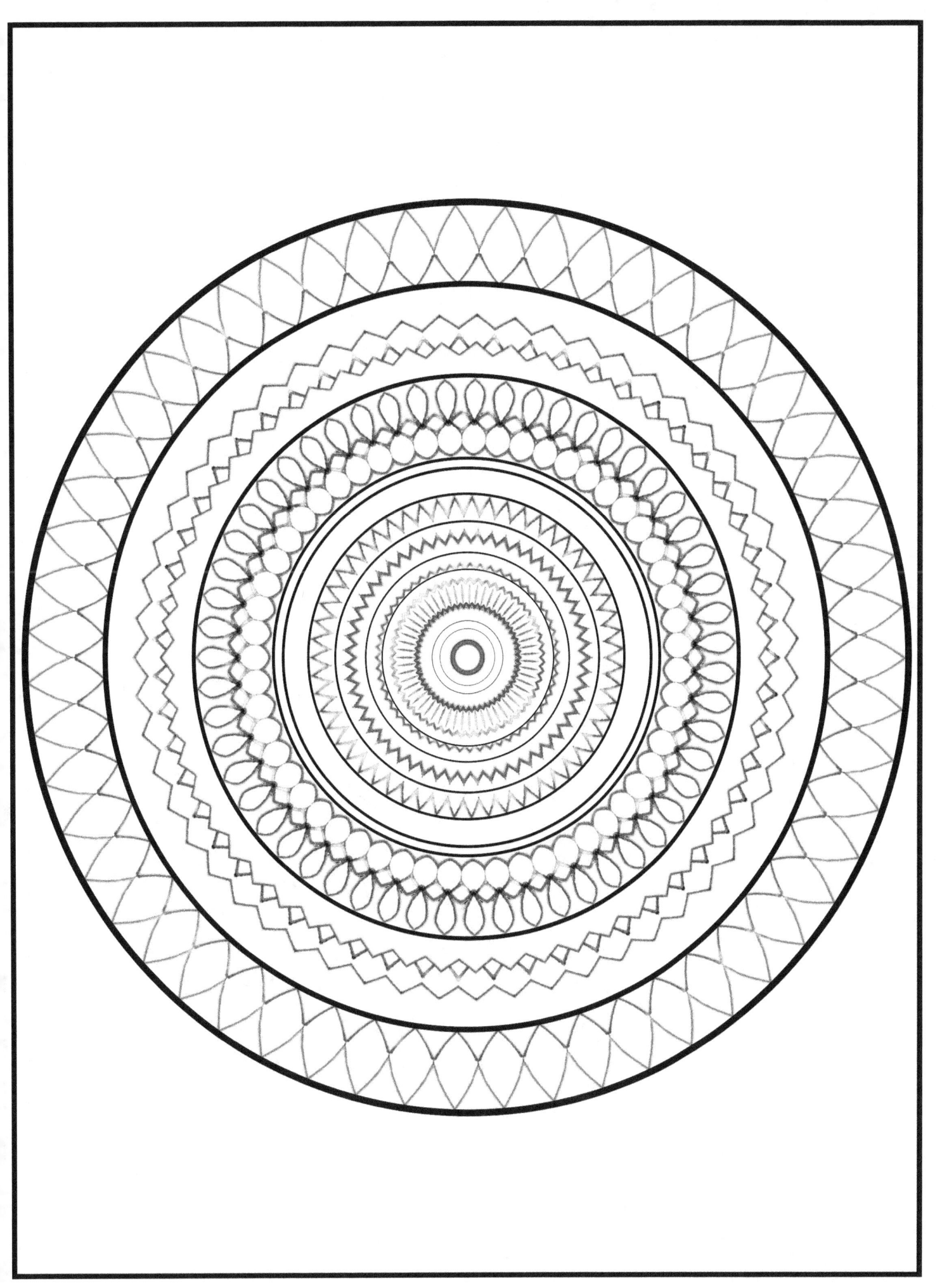

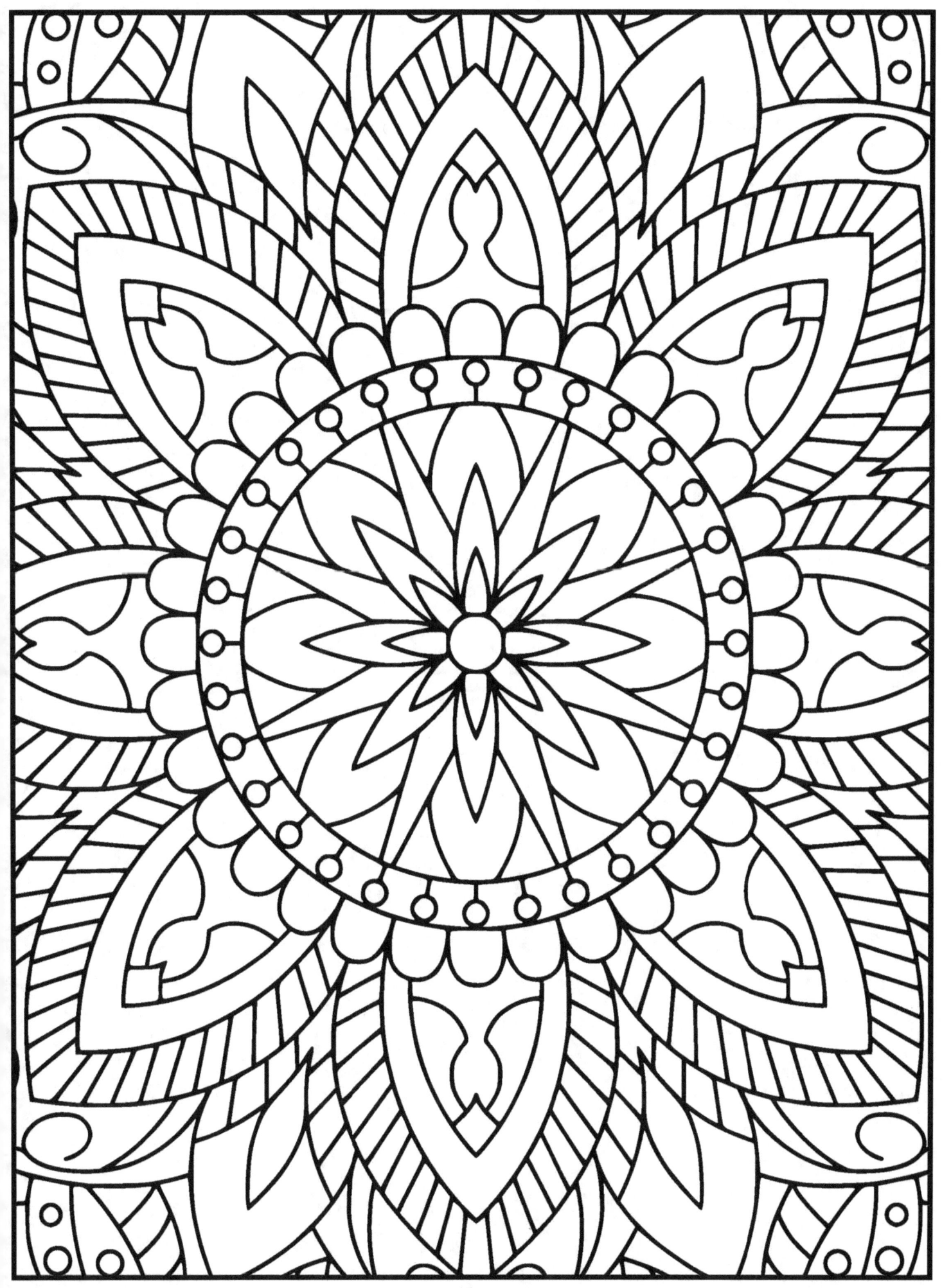

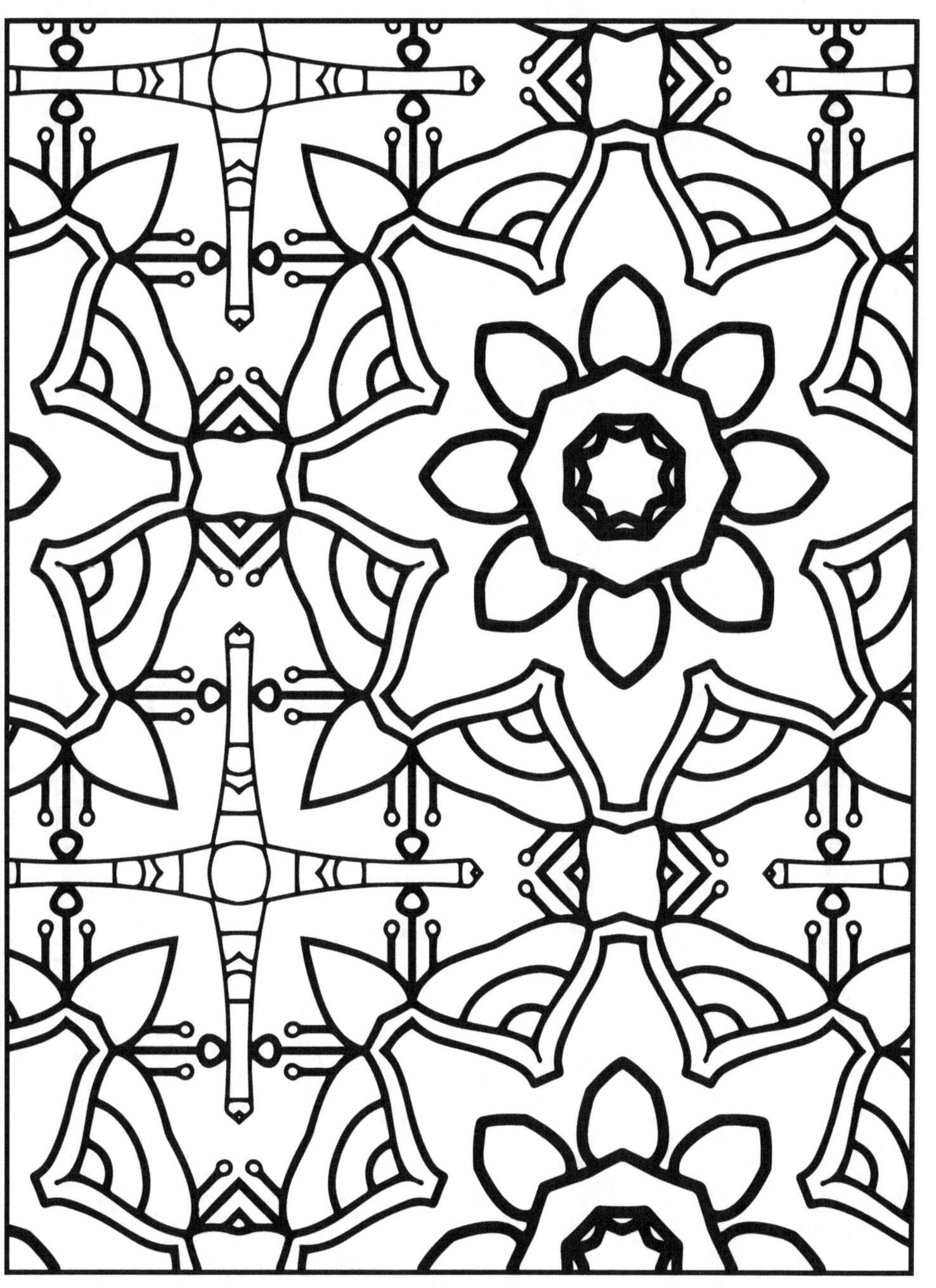

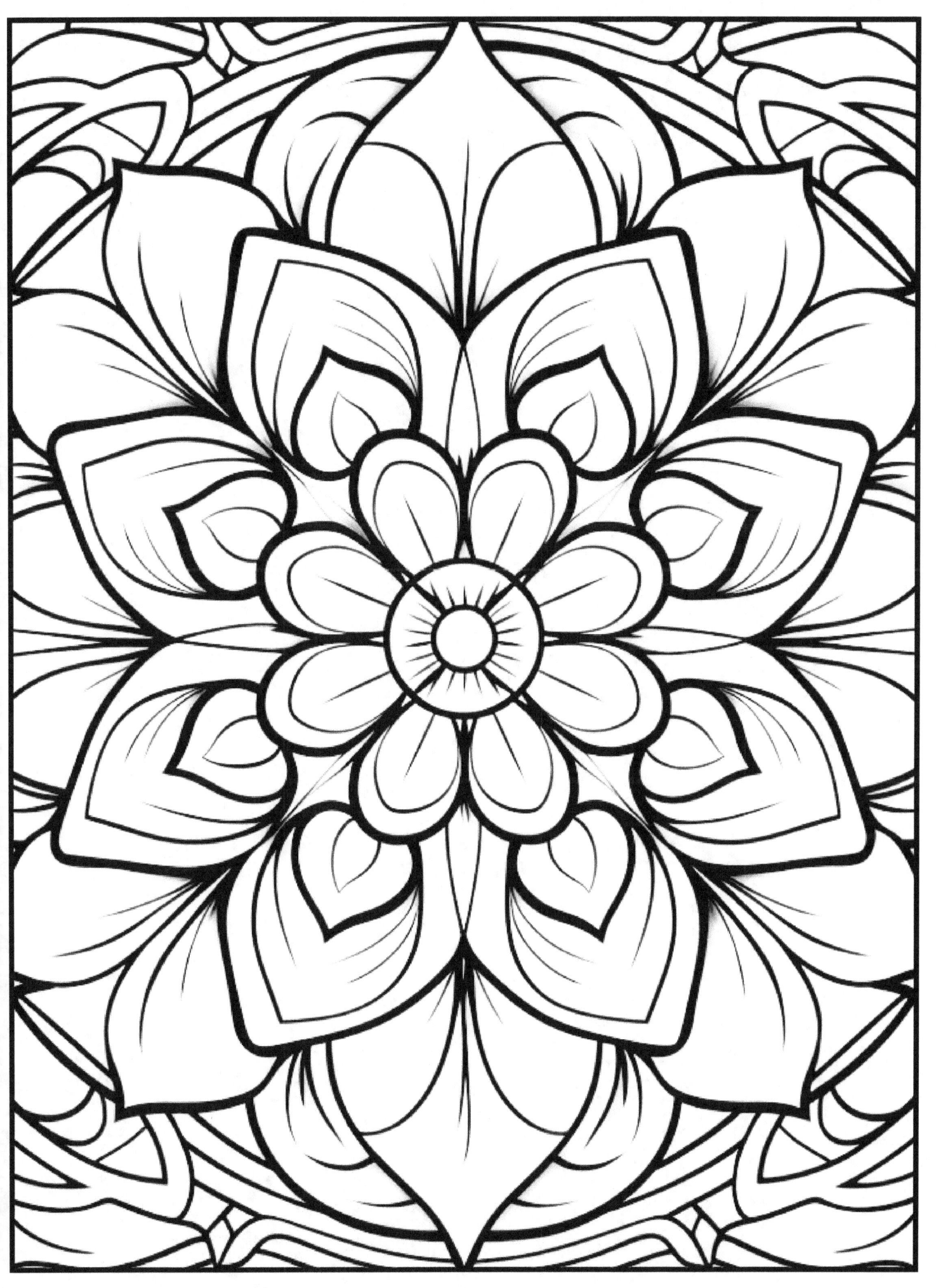

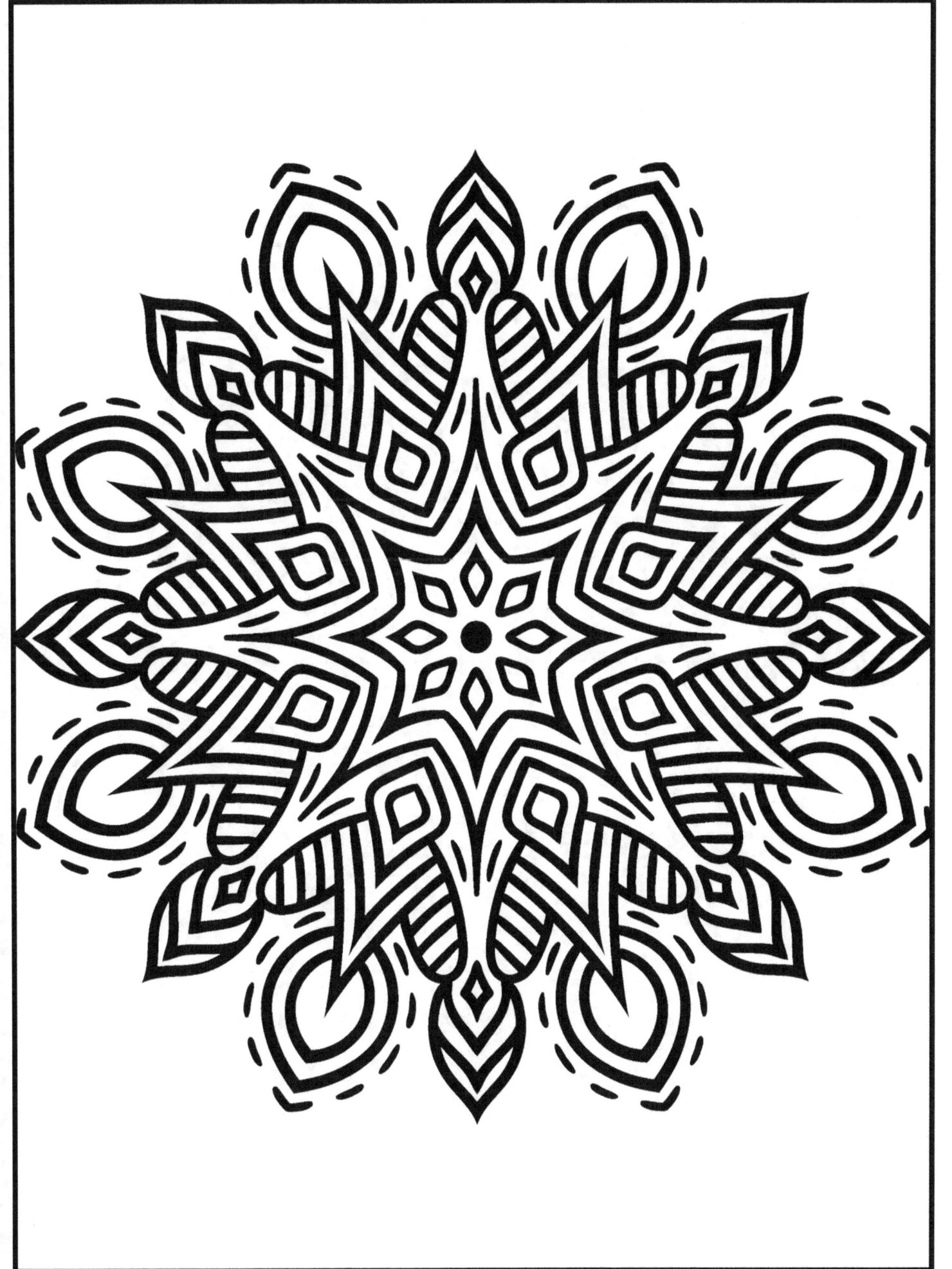

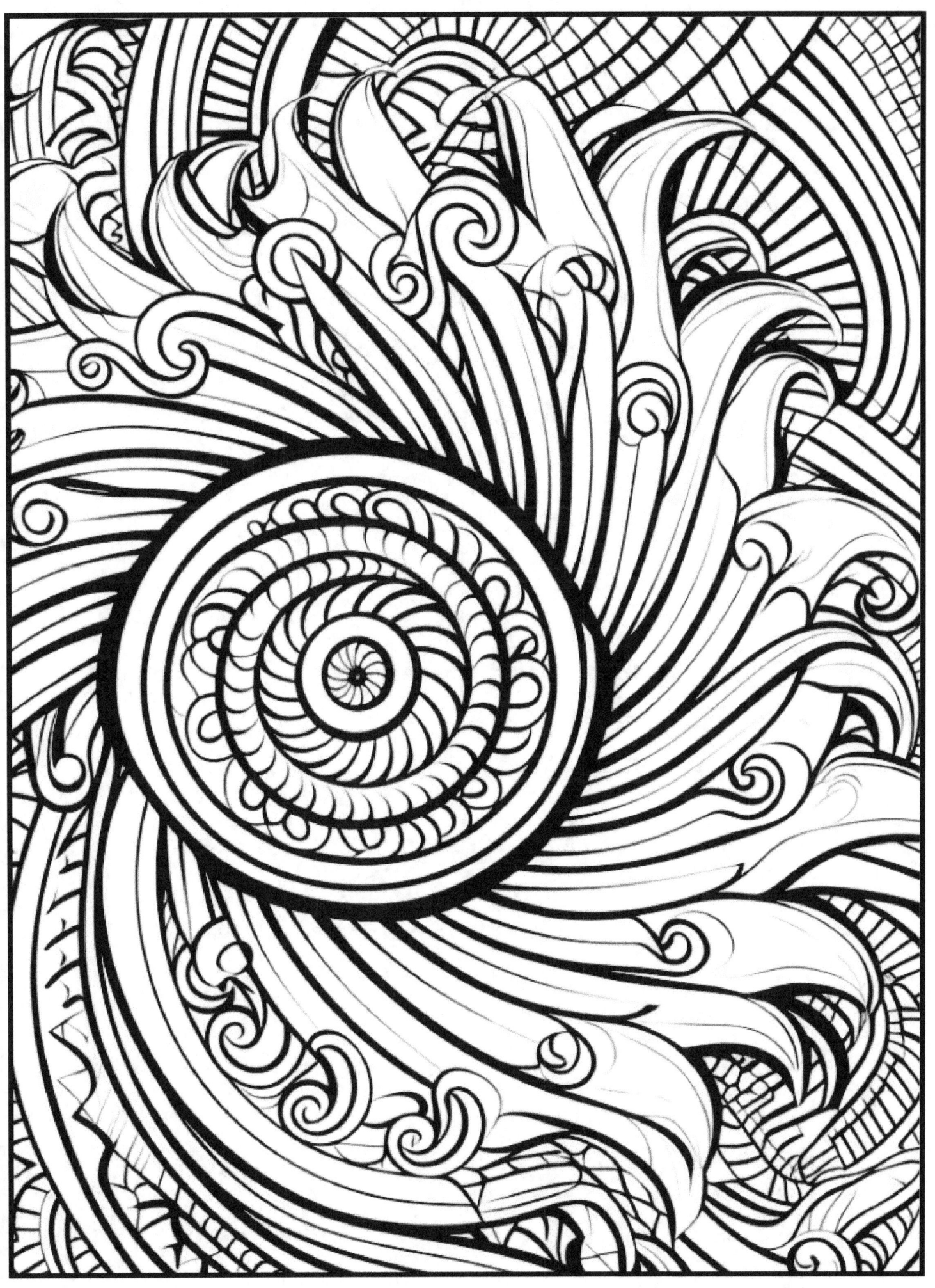

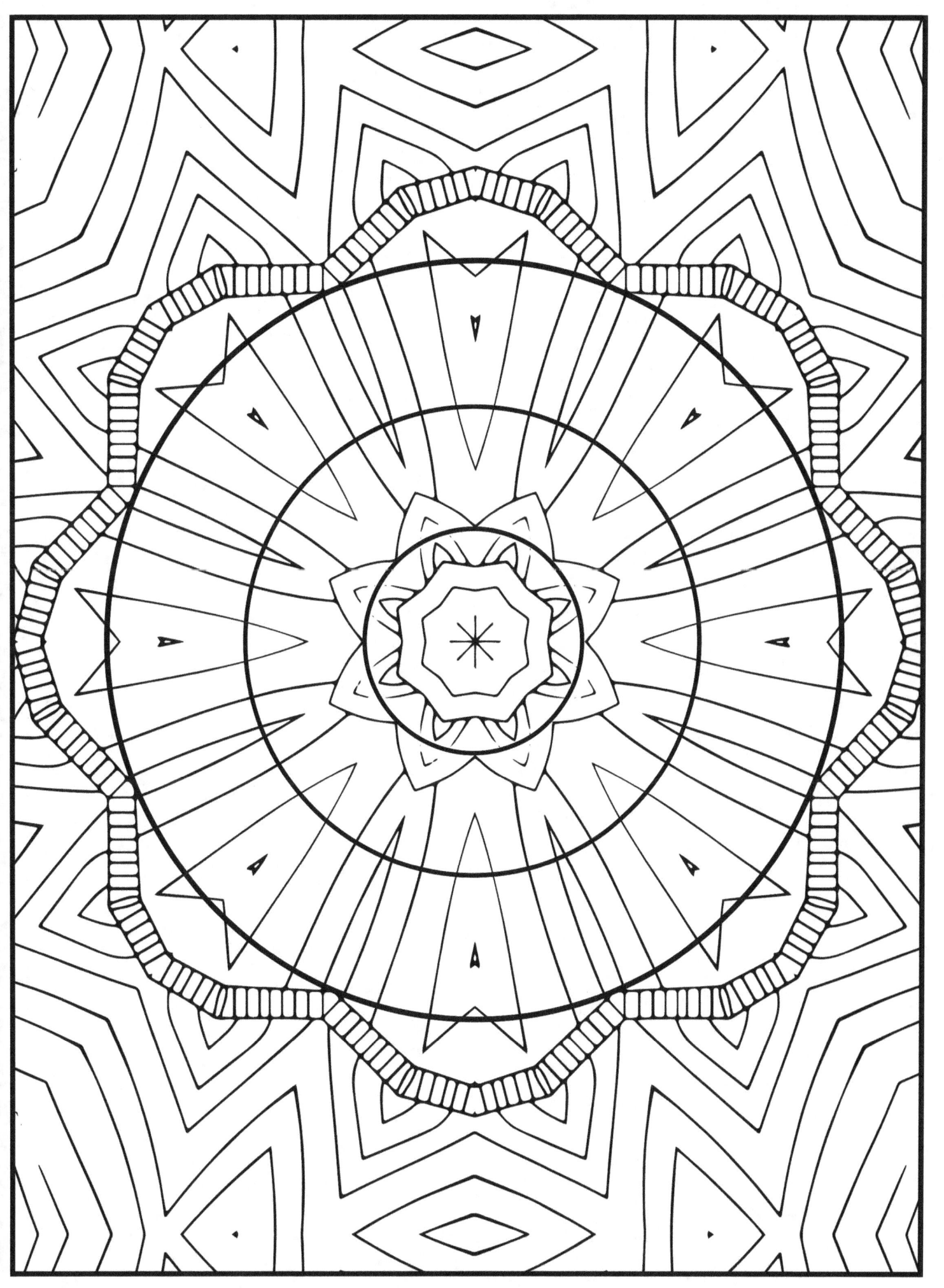

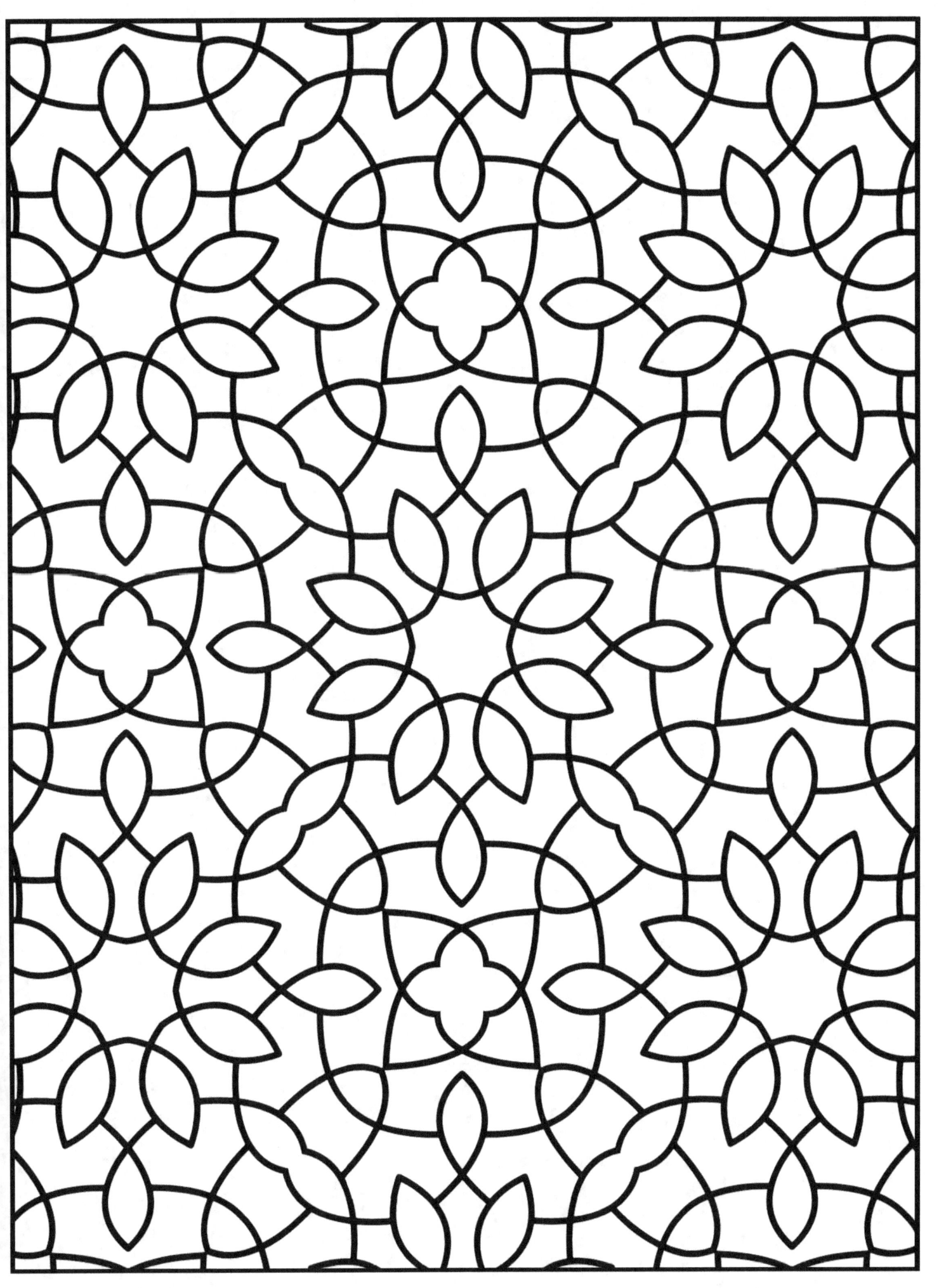

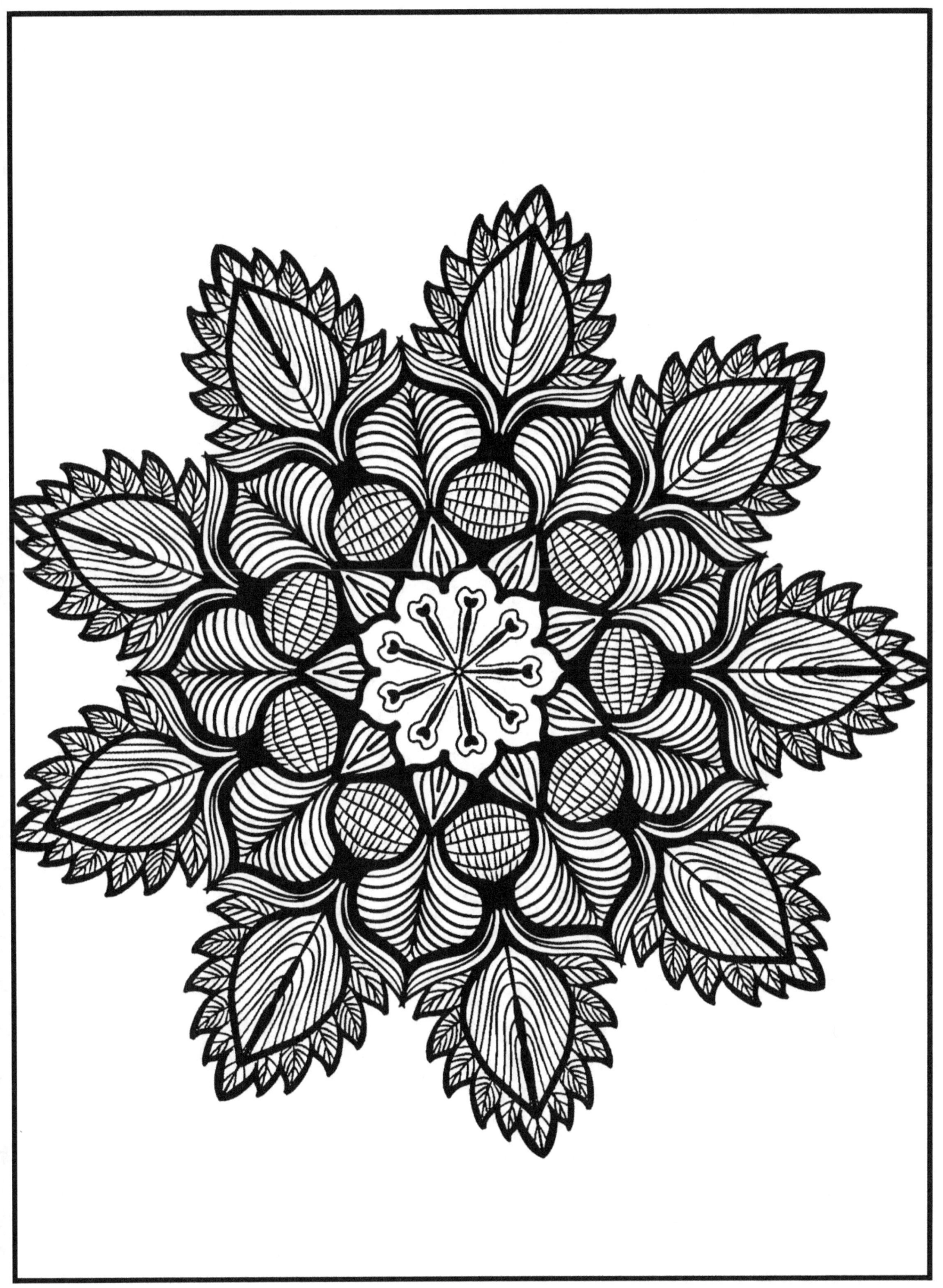

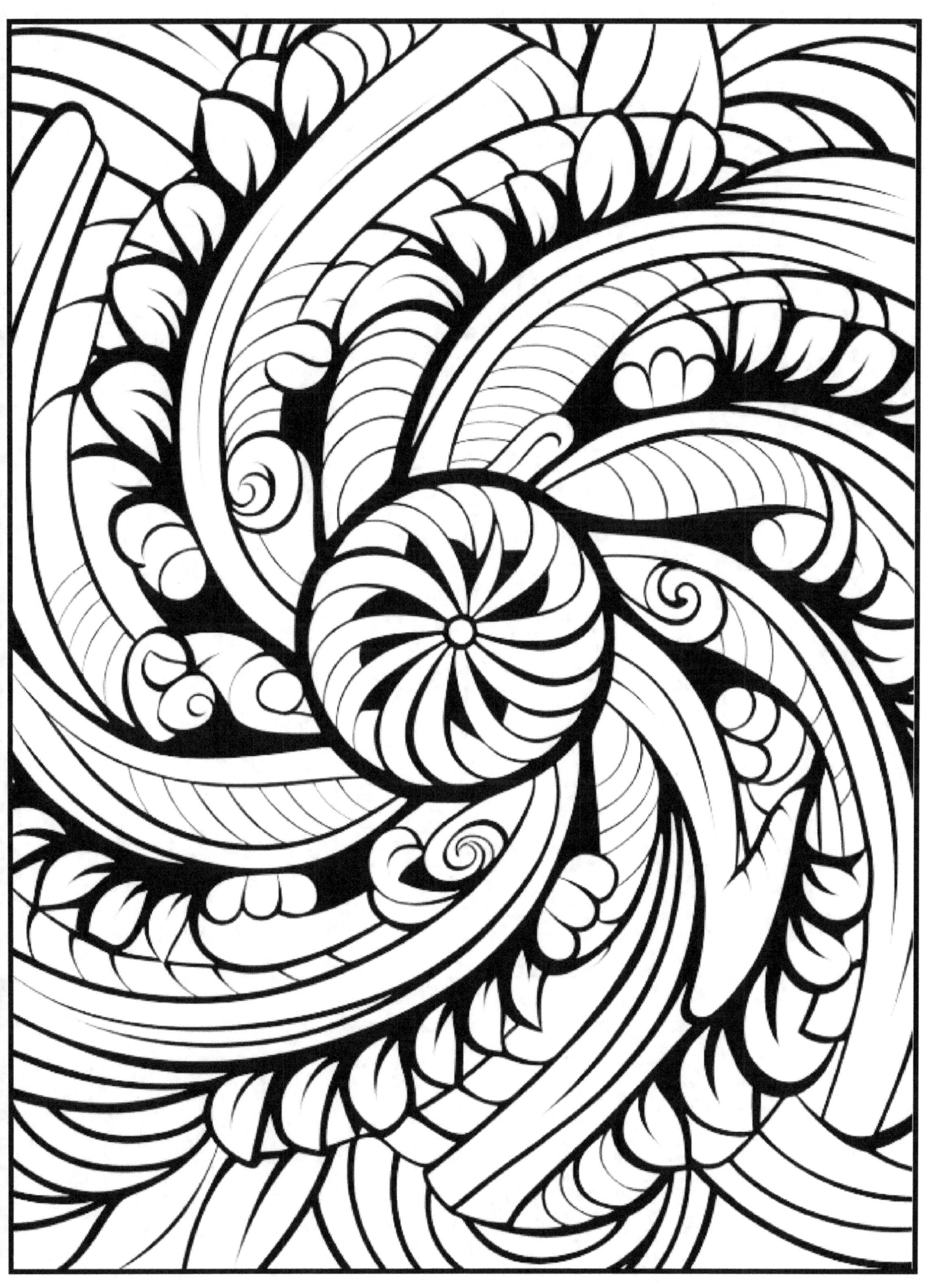

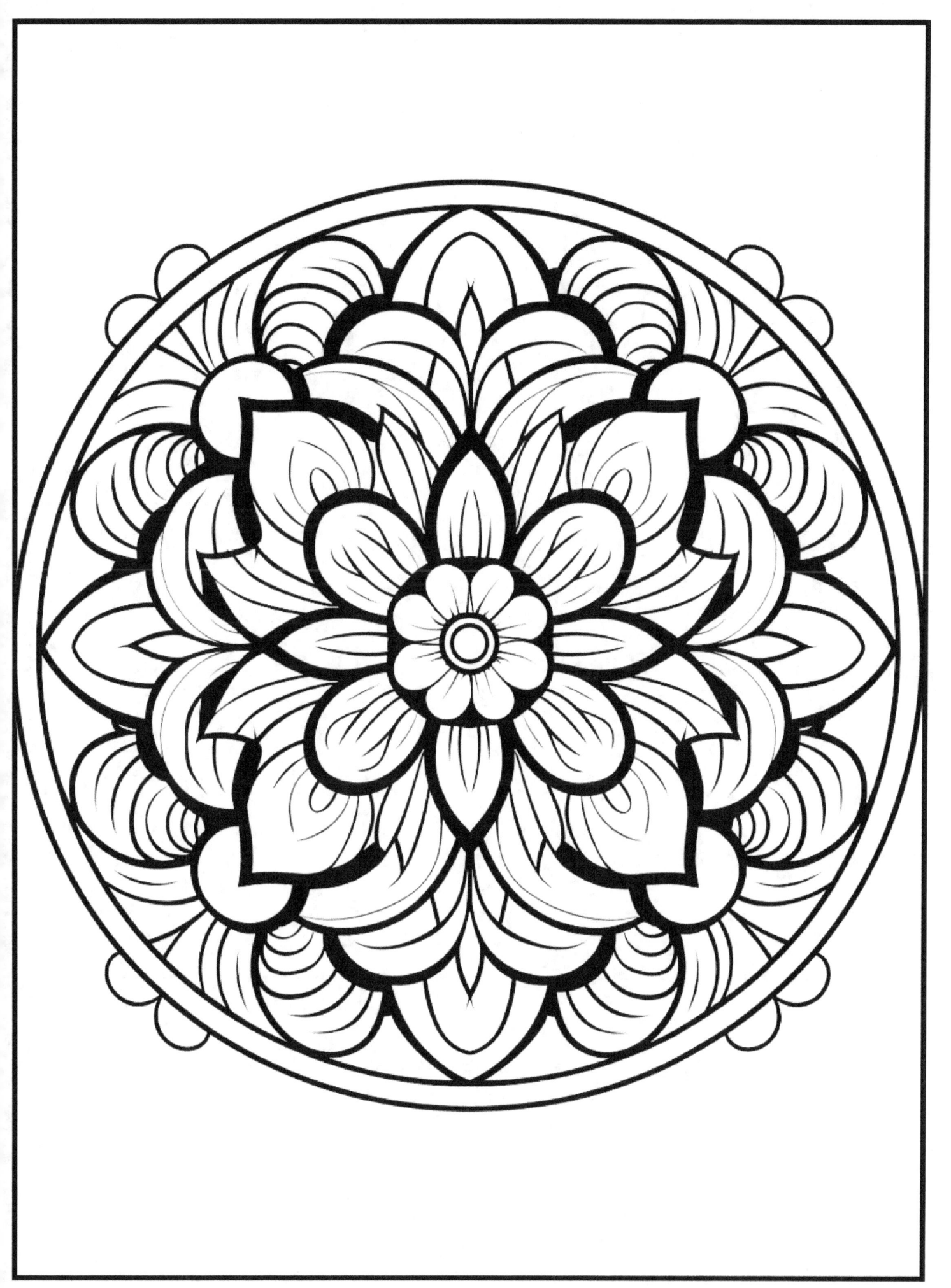

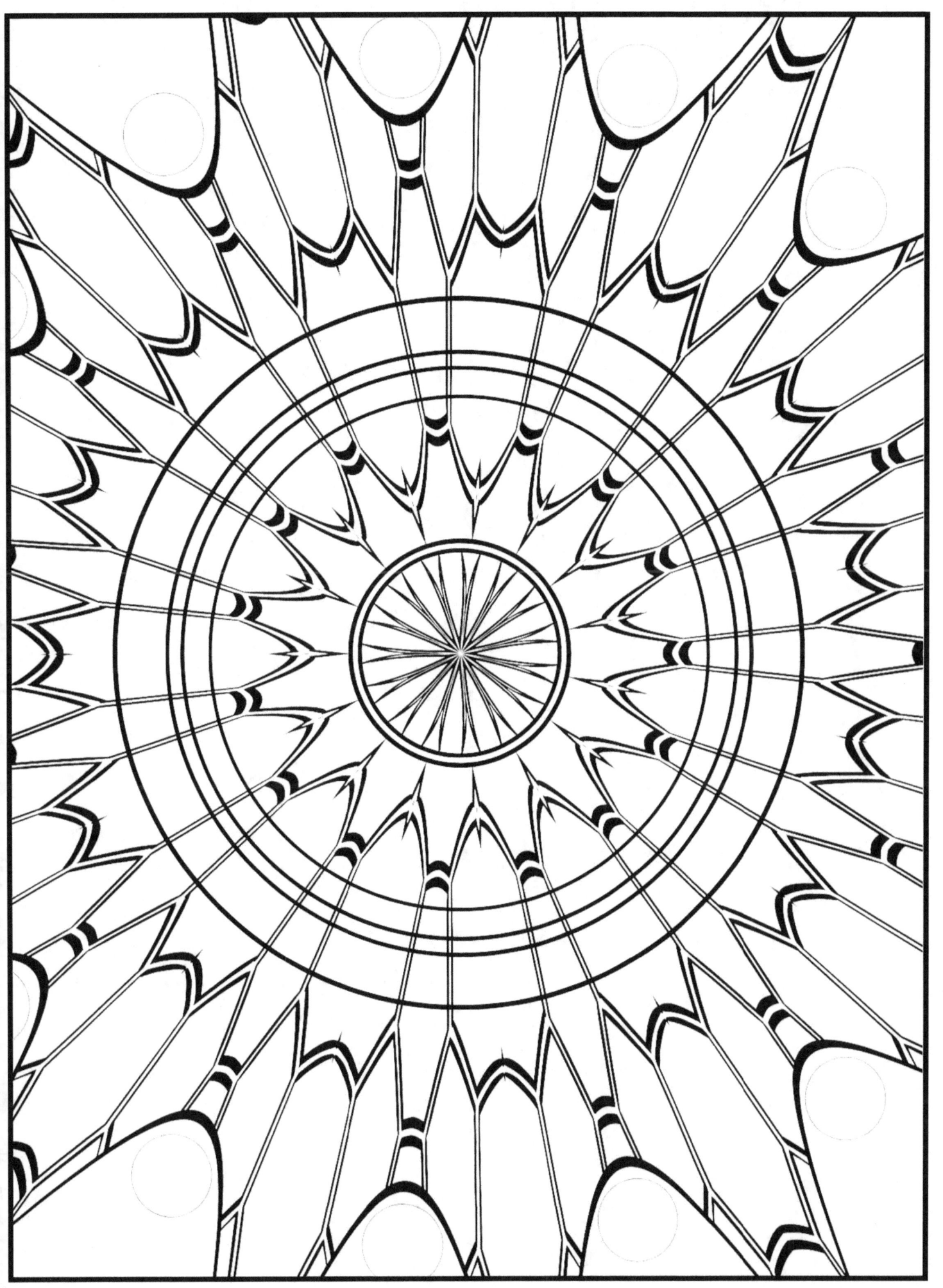

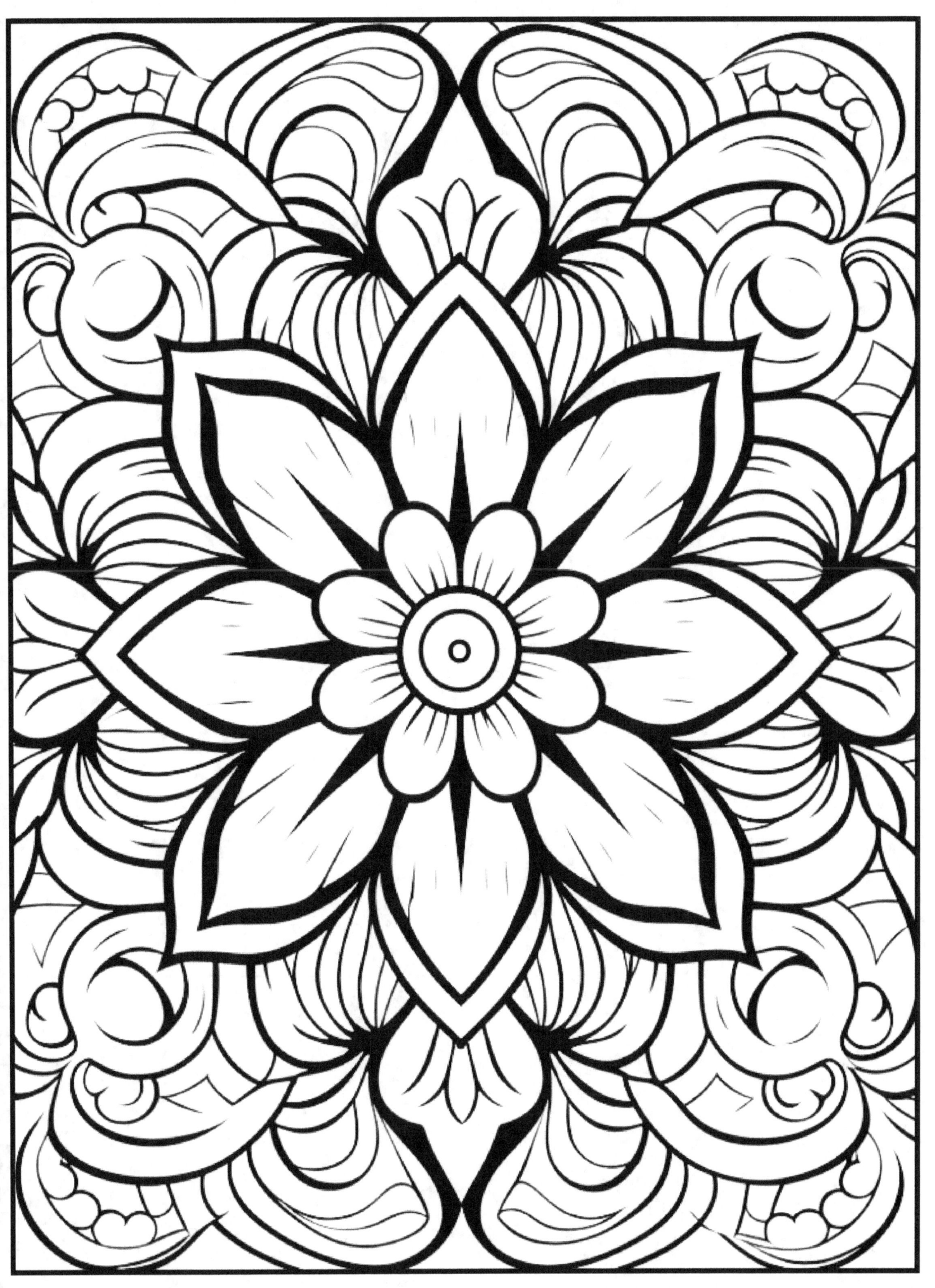

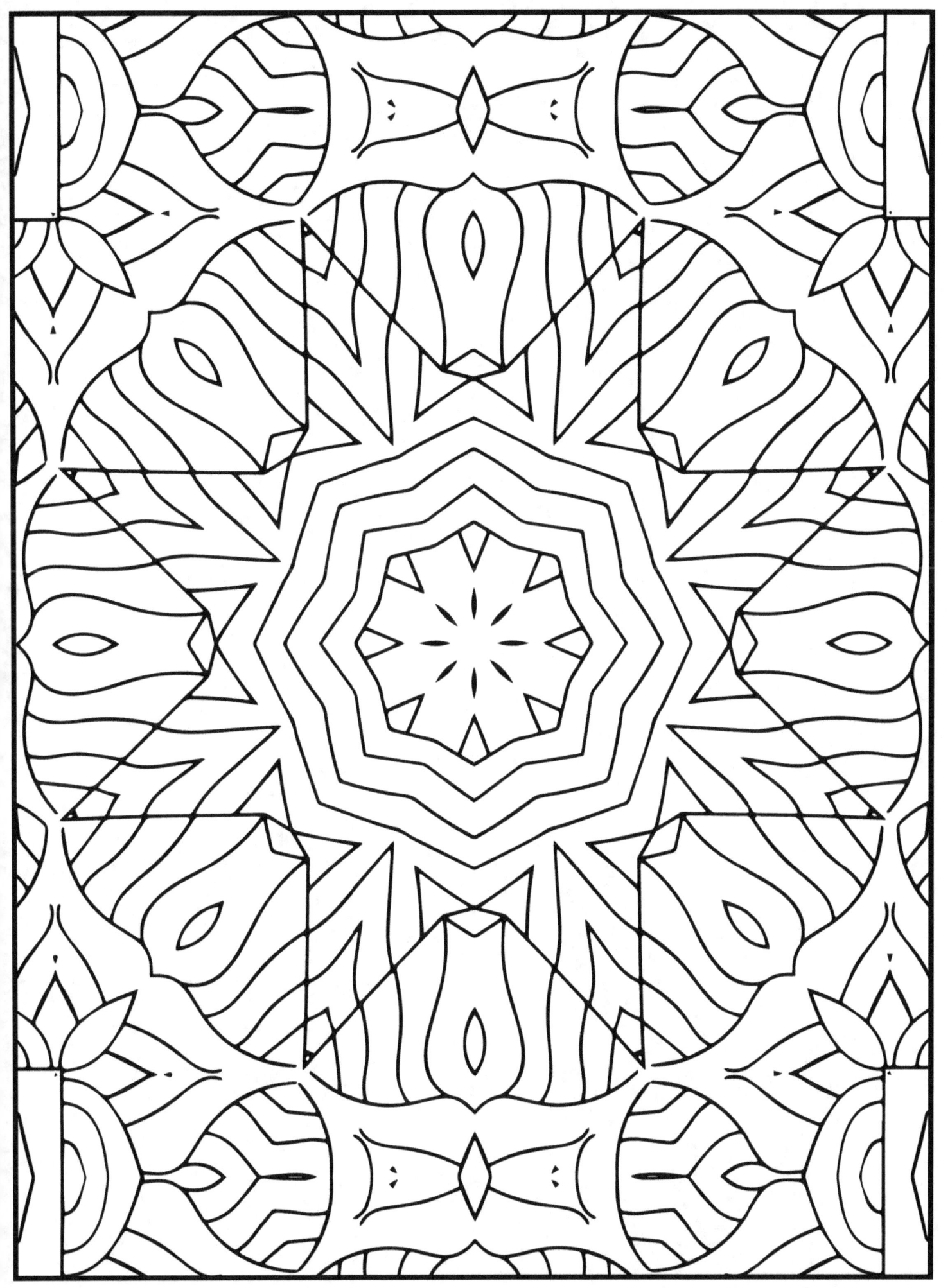

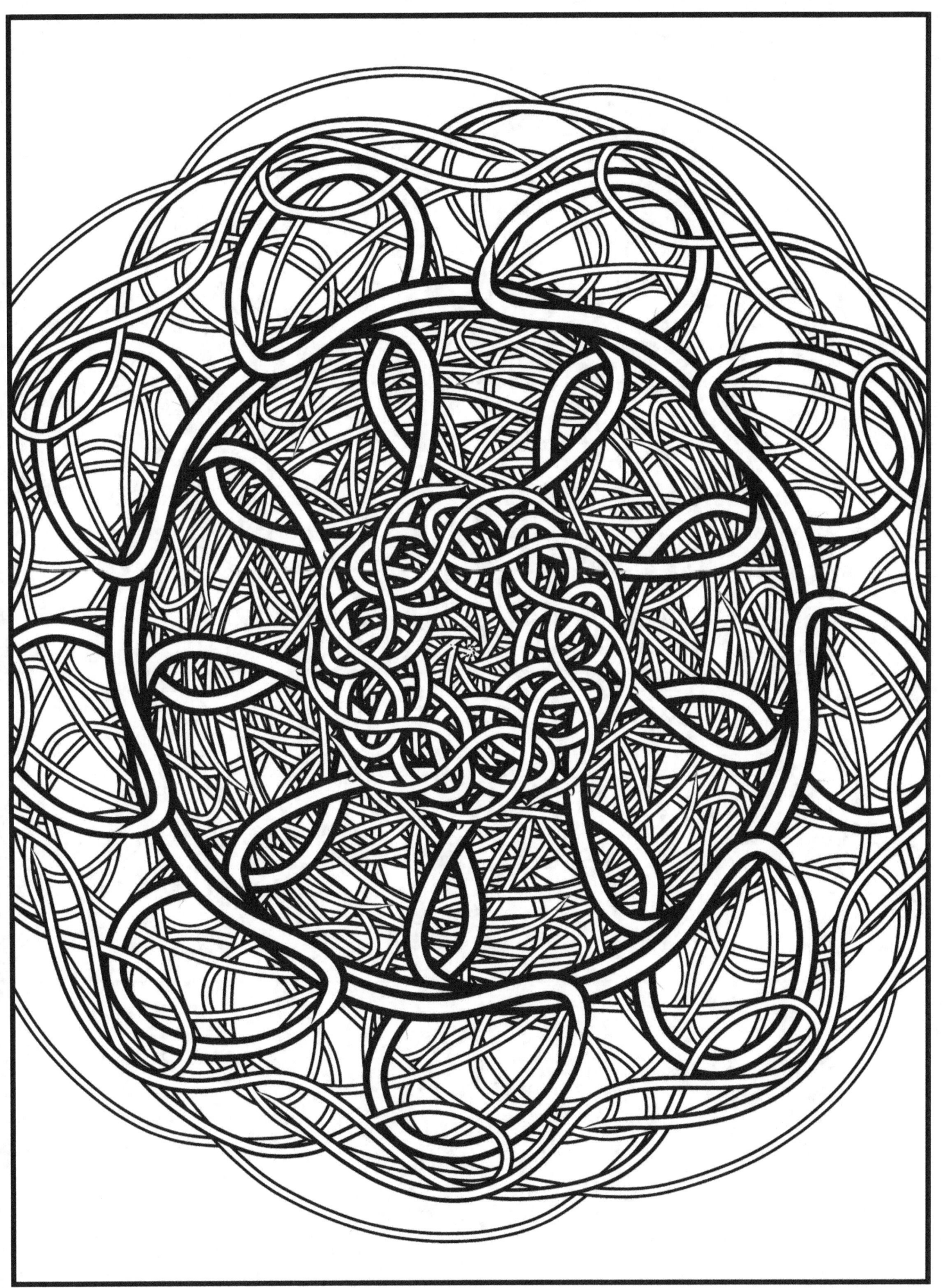

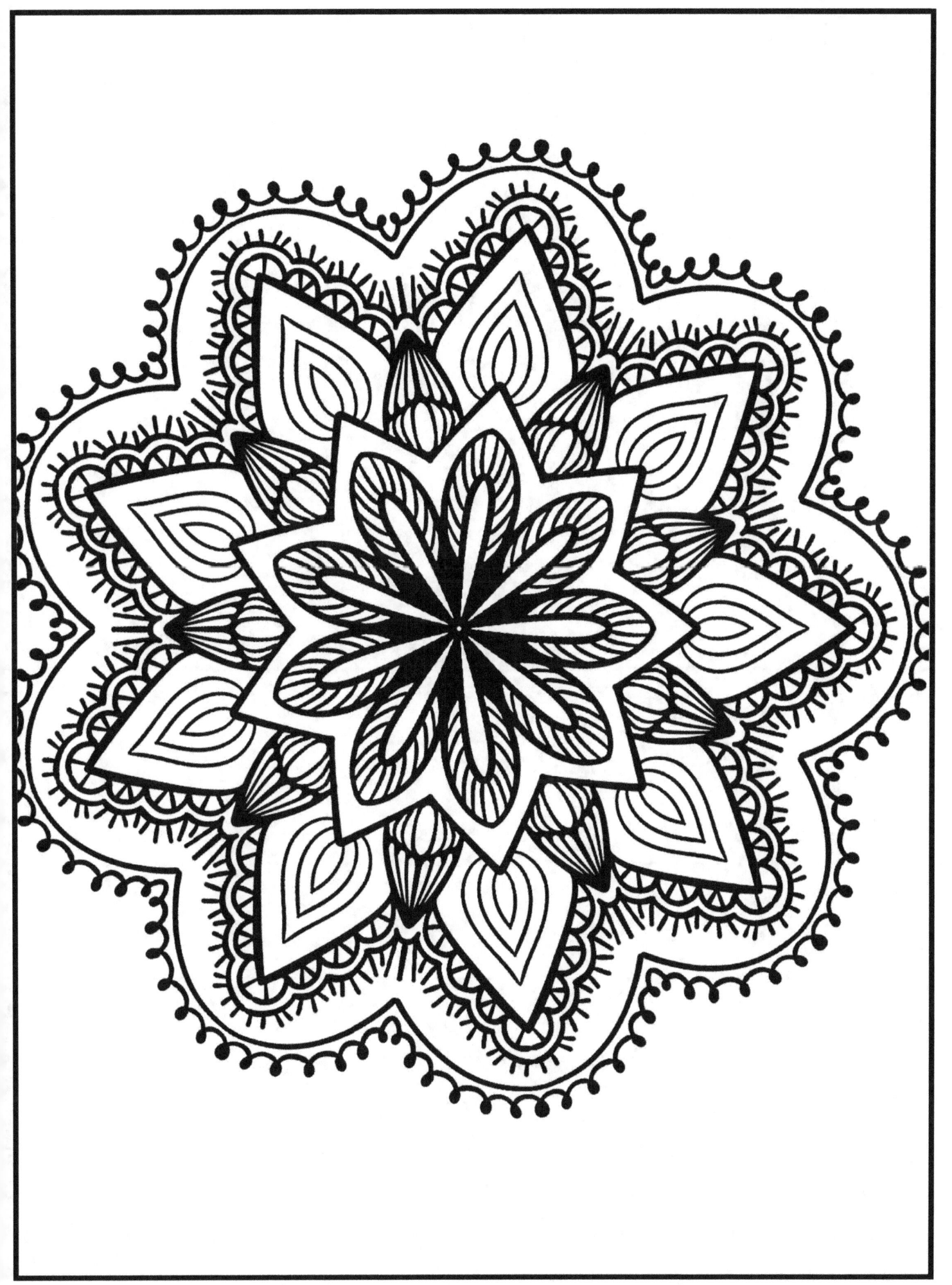

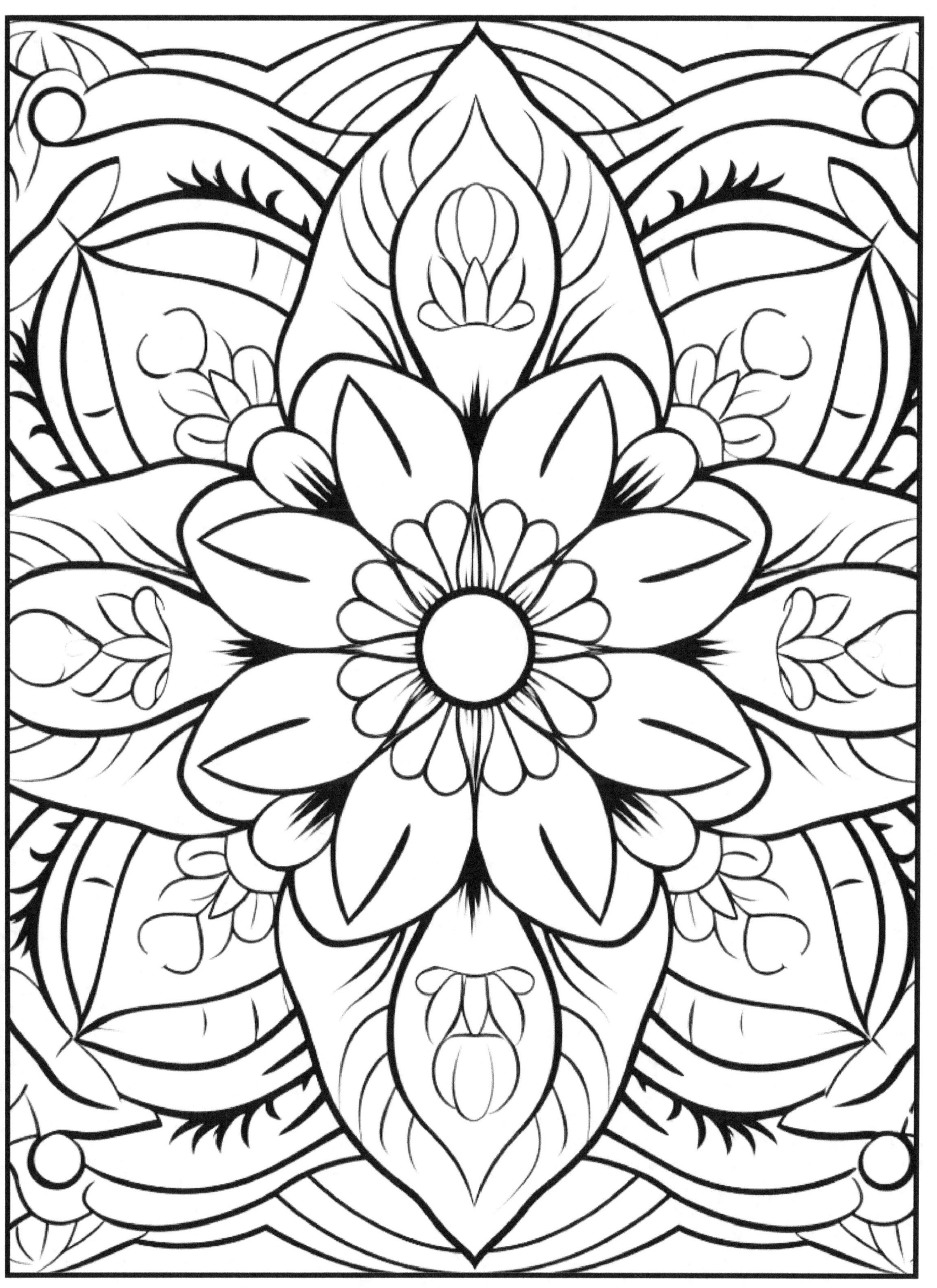

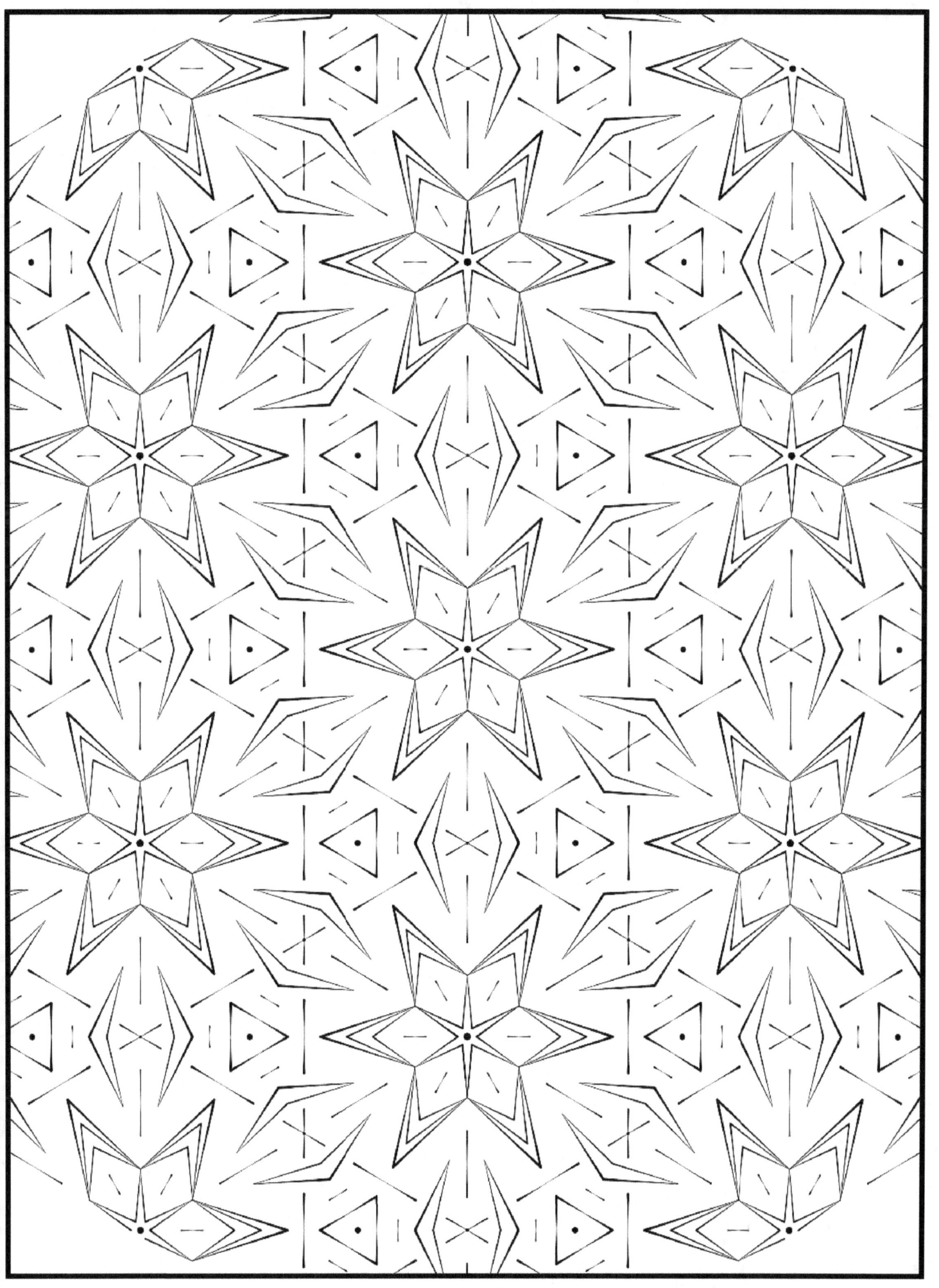

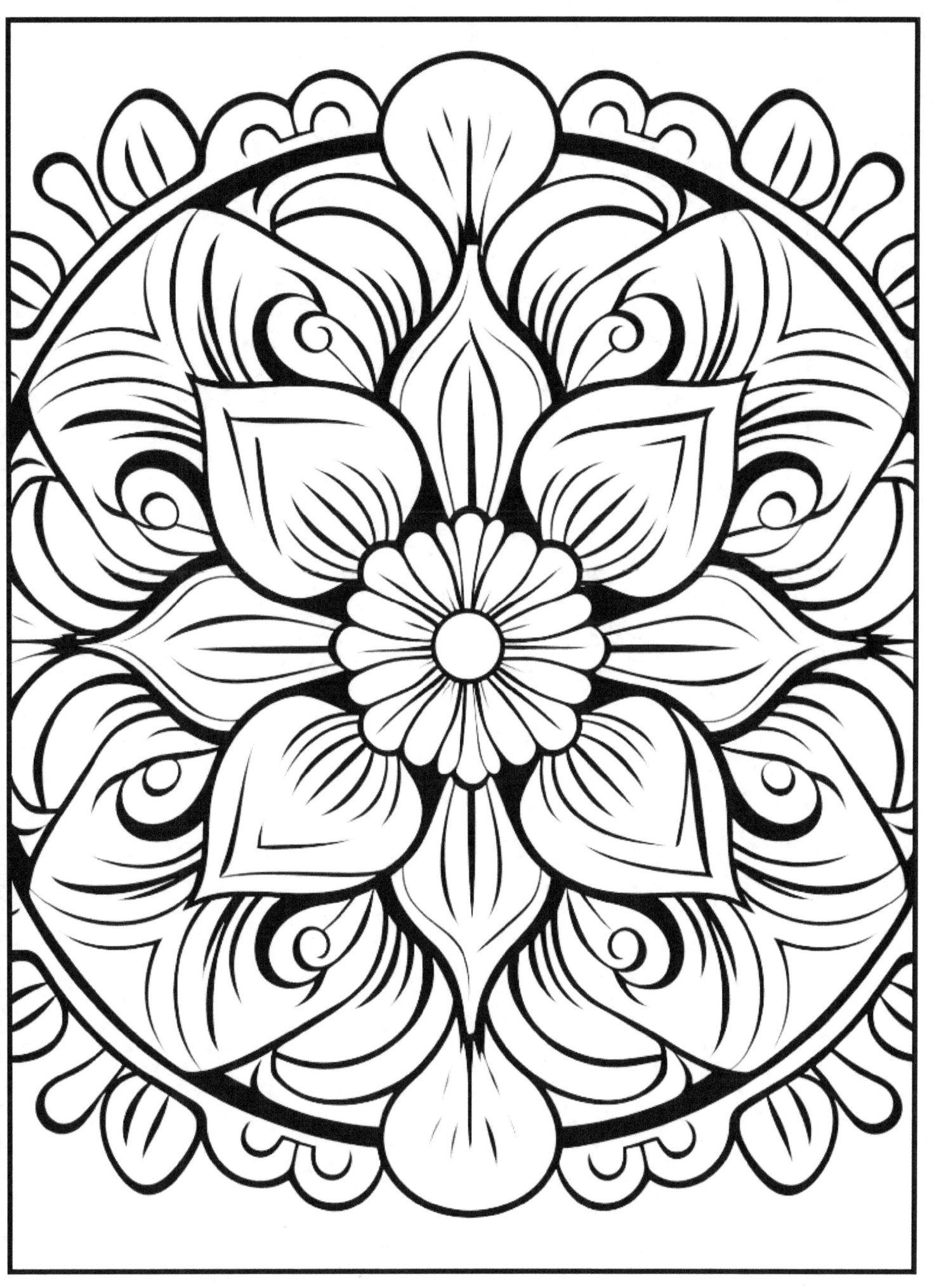

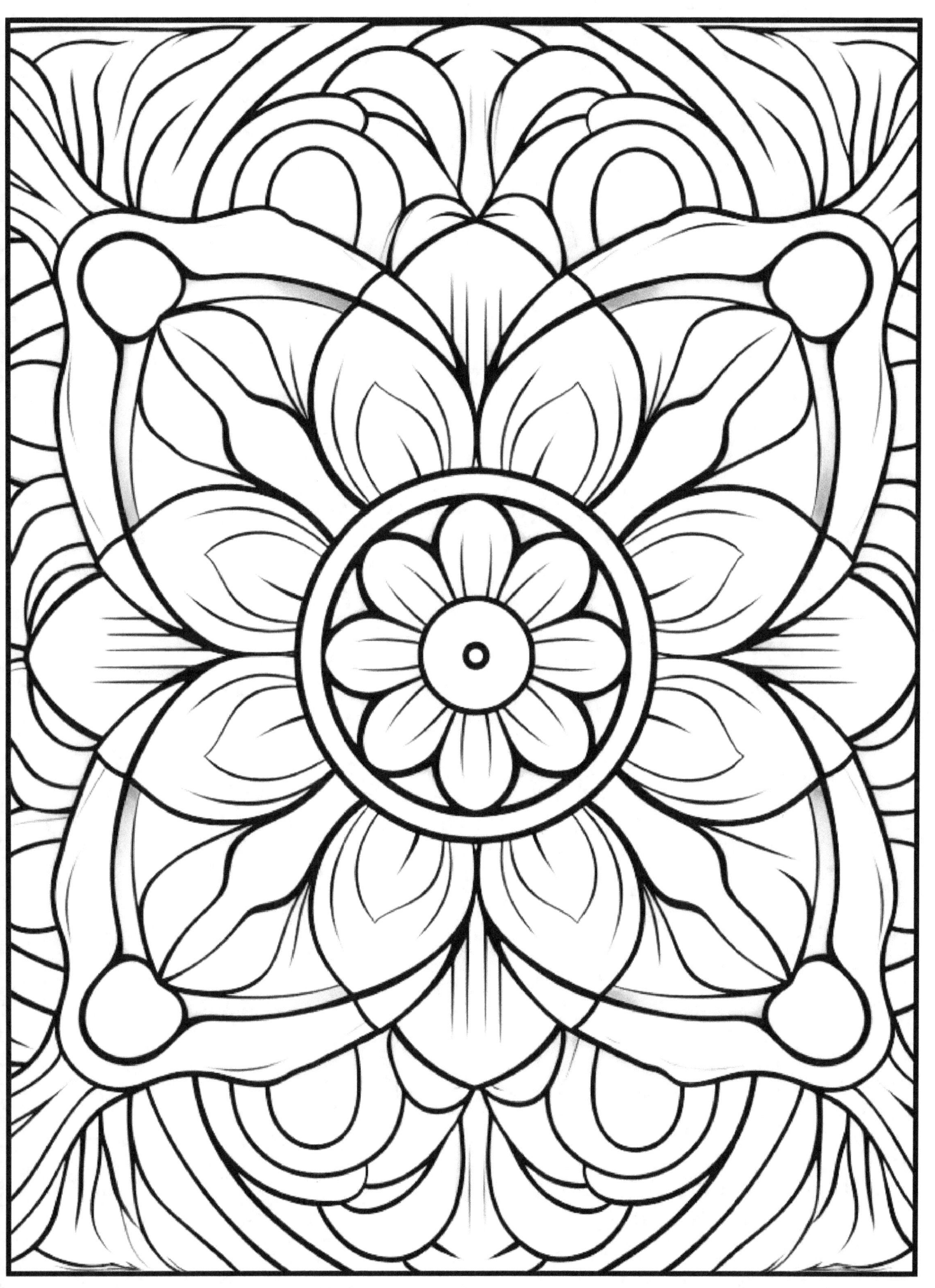

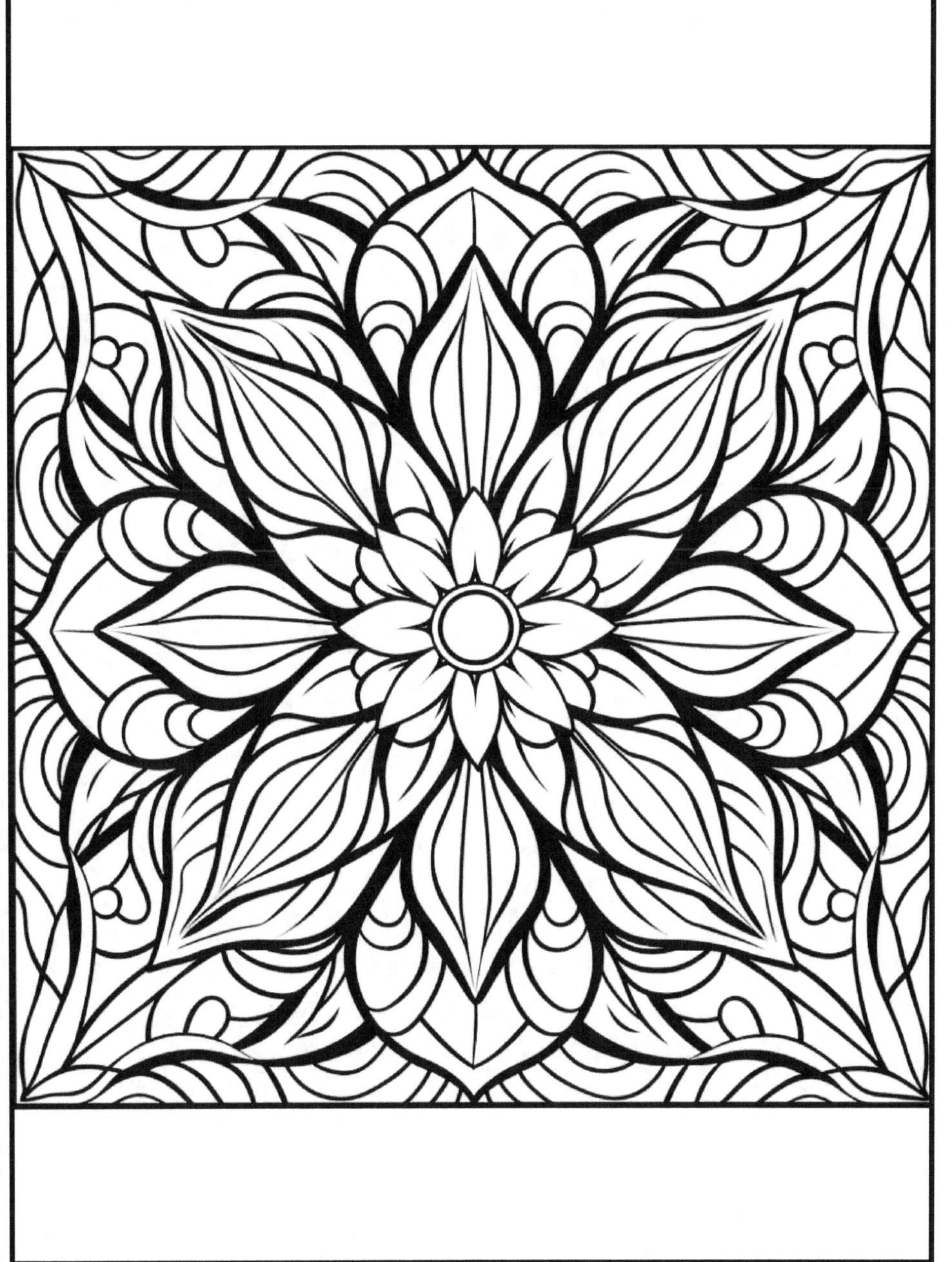

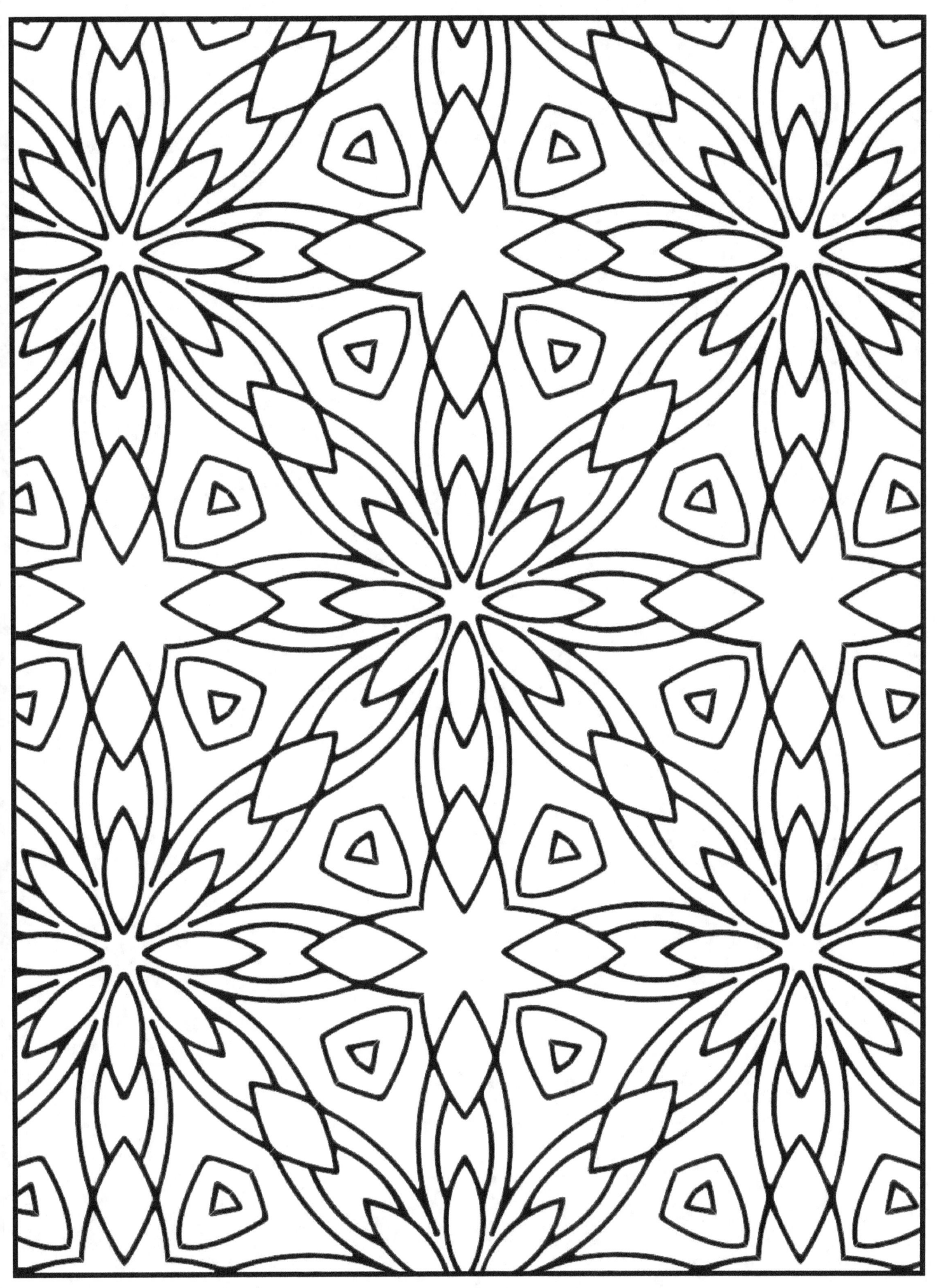

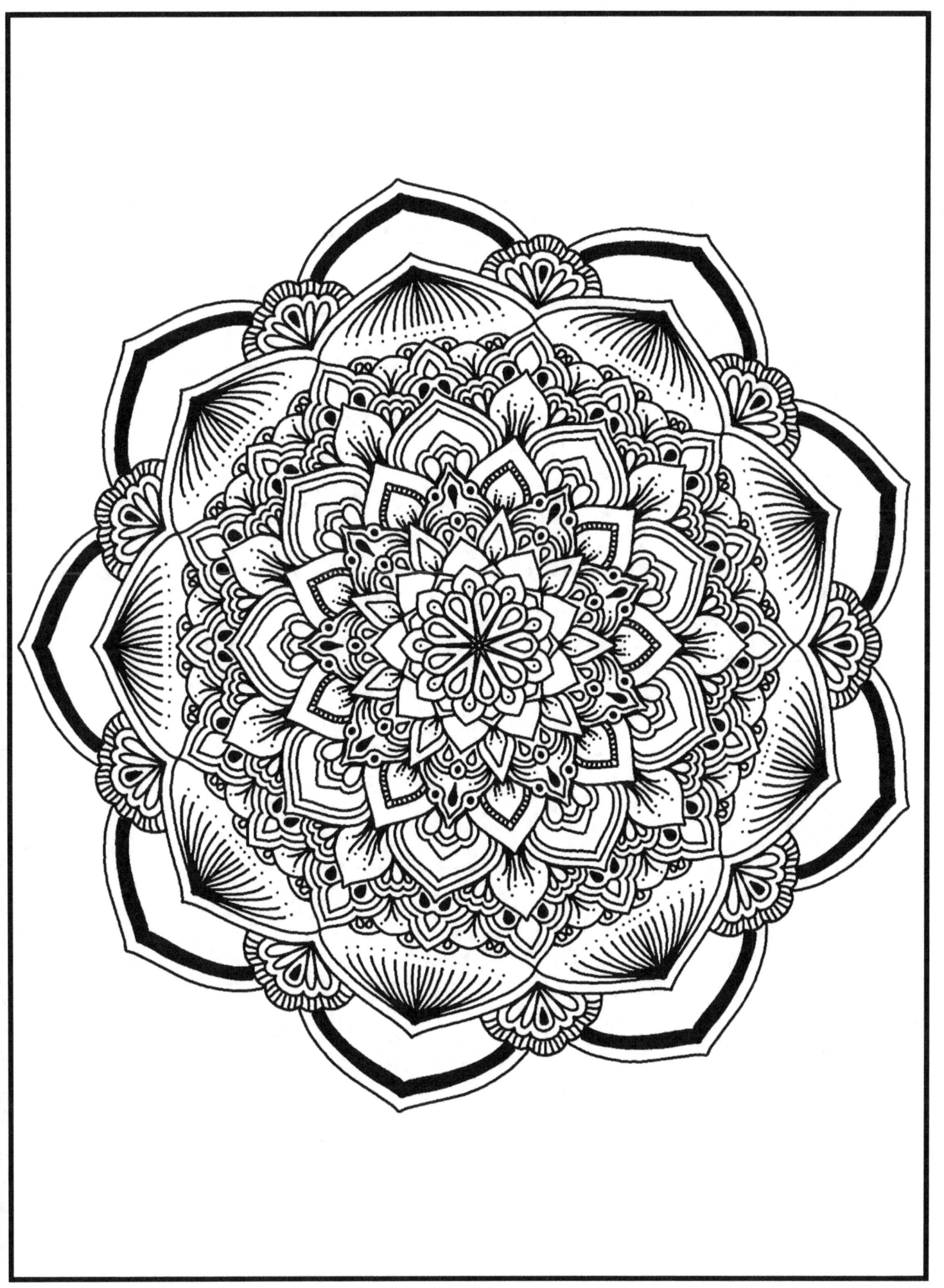

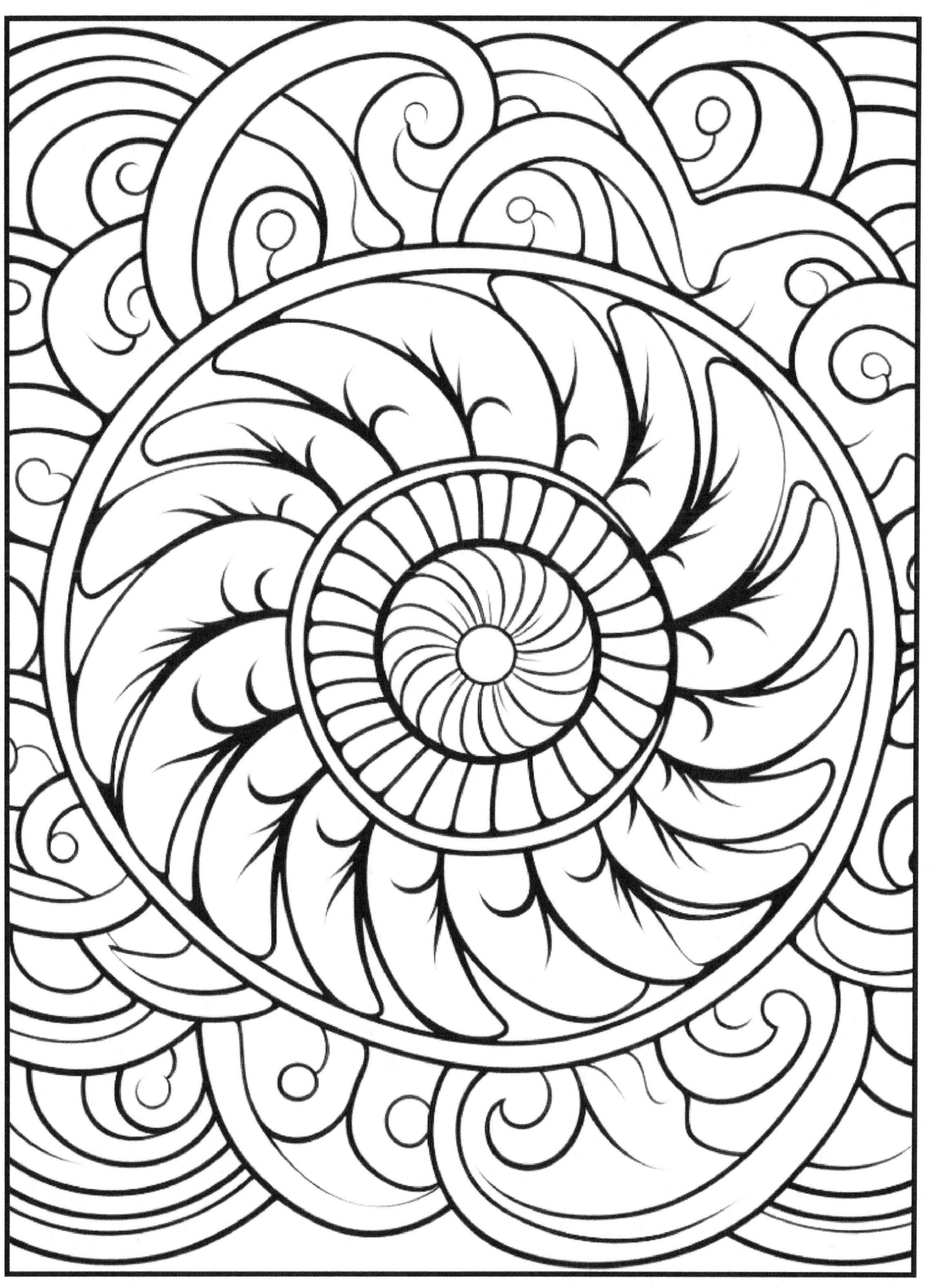

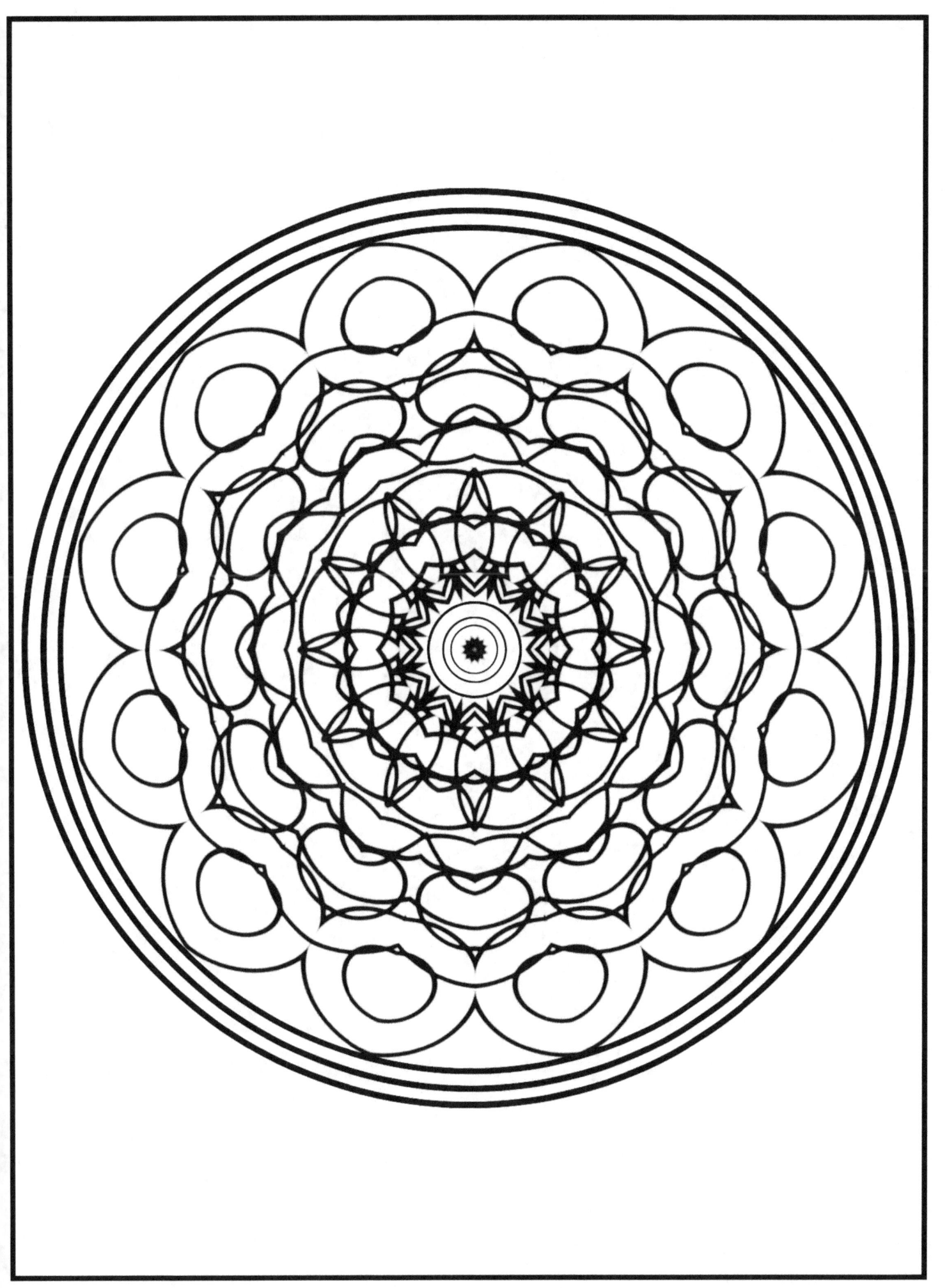

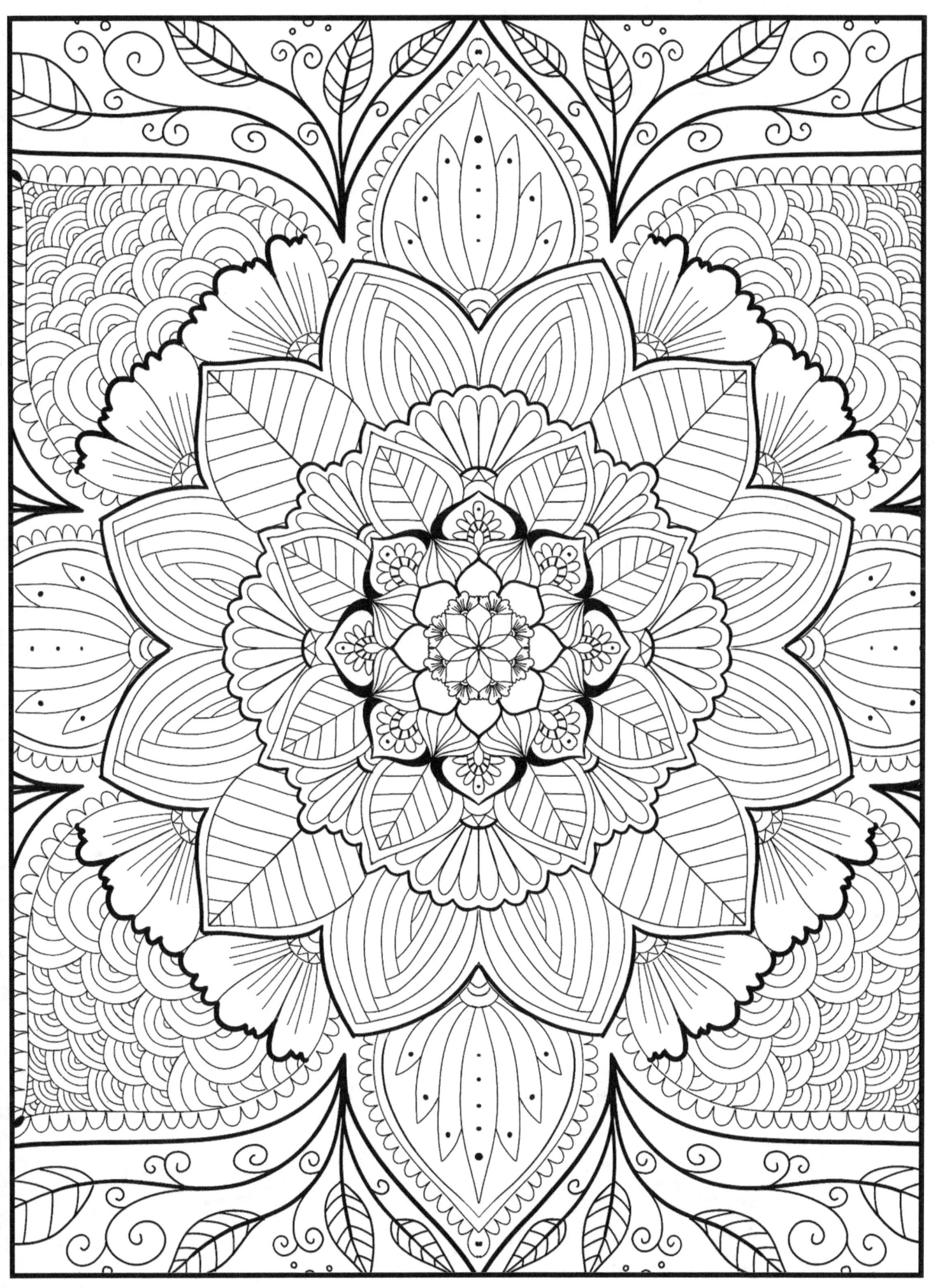

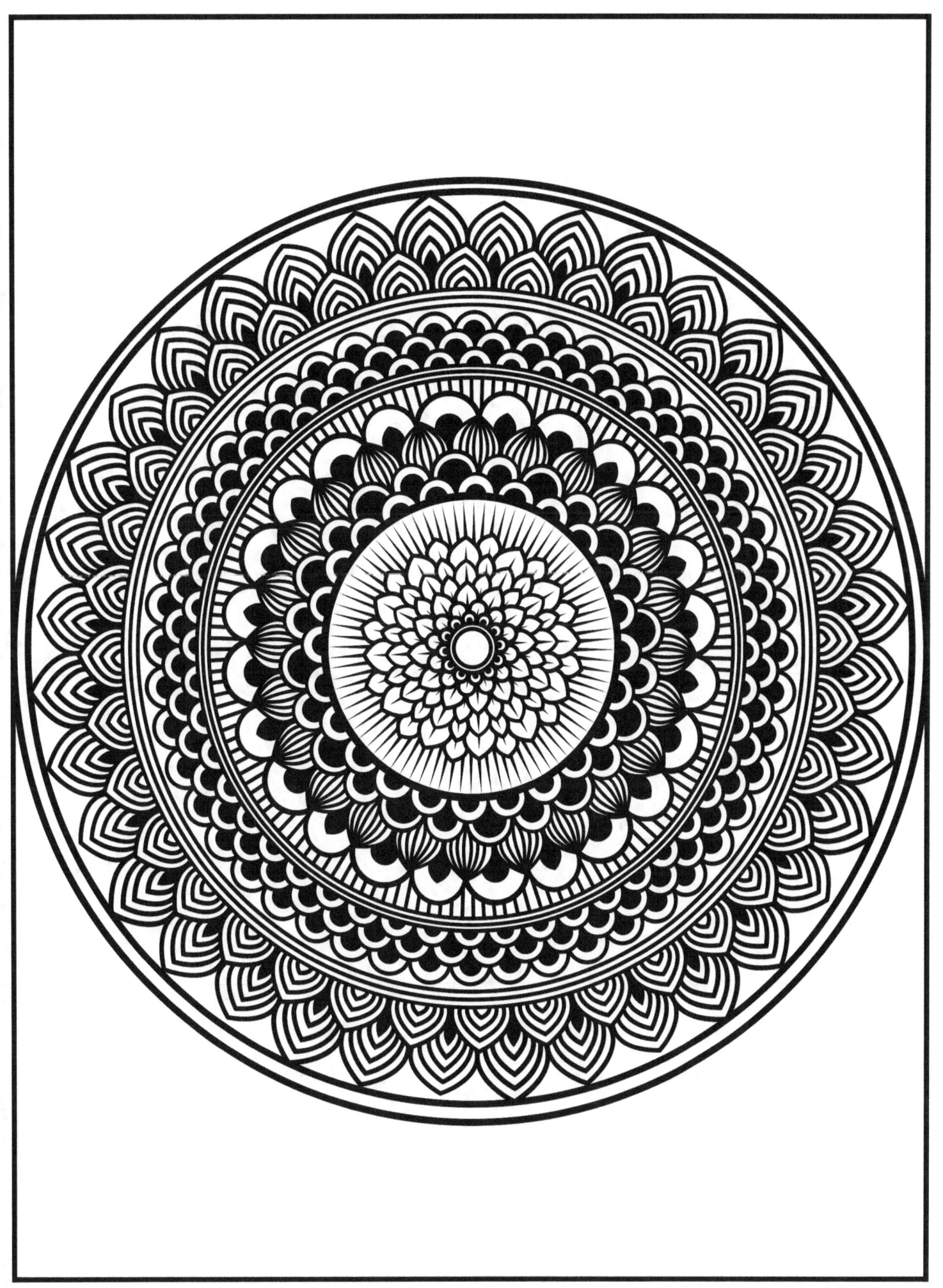

www.ingramcontent.com/pod-product-compliance
Lightning Source LLC
Chambersburg PA
CBHW082219290526
45794CB00009B/3595